THE BASICS OF FINANCIAL MODELING

Jack Avon

The Basics of Financial Modeling

ISBN-13 (pbk): 978-1-4842-0872-4

ISBN-13 (electronic): 978-1-4842-0871-7

Trademarked names, logos, and images may appear in this book. Rather than use a trademark symbol with every occurrence of a trademarked name, logo, or image we use the names, logos, and images only in an editorial fashion and to the benefit of the trademark owner, with no intention of infringement of the trademark.

The use in this publication of trade names, trademarks, service marks, and similar terms, even if they are not identified as such, is not to be taken as an expression of opinion as to whether or not they are subject to proprietary rights.

While the advice and information in this book are believed to be true and accurate at the date of publication, neither the authors nor the editors nor the publisher can accept any legal responsibility for any errors or omissions that may be made. The publisher makes no warranty, express or implied, with respect to the material contained herein.

Distributed to the book trade worldwide by Springer Science+Business Media New York, 233 Spring Street, 6th Floor, New York, NY 10013. Phone 1-800-SPRINGER, fax (201) 348-4505, e-mail orders-ny@springer-sbm.com, or visit www.springeronline.com. Apress Media, LLC is a California LLC and the sole member (owner) is Springer Science + Business Media Finance Inc (SSBM Finance Inc). SSBM Finance Inc is a **Delaware** corporation.

For information on translations, please e-mail rights@apress.com, or visit www.apress.com.

Apress and friends of ED books may be purchased in bulk for academic, corporate, or promotional use. eBook versions and licenses are also available for most titles. For more information, reference our Special Bulk Sales–eBook Licensing web page at www.apress.com/bulk-sales.

Any source code or other supplementary materials referenced by the author in this text is available to readers at www.apress.com. For detailed information about how to locate your book's source code, go to www.apress.com/source-code/.

Apress Business: The Unbiased Source of Business Information

Apress business books provide essential information and practical advice, each written for practitioners by recognized experts. Busy managers and professionals in all areas of the business world—and at all levels of technical sophistication—look to our books for the actionable ideas and tools they need to solve problems, update and enhance their professional skills, make their work lives easier, and capitalize on opportunity.

Whatever the topic on the business spectrum—entrepreneurship, finance, sales, marketing, management, regulation, information technology, among others—Apress has been praised for providing the objective information and unbiased advice you need to excel in your daily work life. Our authors have no axes to grind; they understand they have one job only—to deliver up-to-date, accurate information simply, concisely, and with deep insight that addresses the real needs of our readers.

It is increasingly hard to find information—whether in the news media, on the Internet, and now all too often in books—that is even-handed and has your best interests at heart. We therefore hope that you enjoy this book, which has been carefully crafted to meet our standards of quality and unbiased coverage.

We are always interested in your feedback or ideas for new titles. Perhaps you'd even like to write a book yourself. Whatever the case, reach out to us at editorial@apress.com and an editor will respond swiftly. Incidentally, at the back of this book, you will find a list of useful related titles. Please visit us at www.apress.com to sign up for newsletters and discounts on future purchases.

The Apress Business Team

This book is dedicated to the people through my life who have given me the insight and courage to persist with using computer technology and inspired me to reach for the skies. I would particularly like to thank my original mentor, the late Hugh Blake, who gave me so much of his time to show me where my future, and to Bill Gates, who has been an inspirational human being for most of life.

Contents

About the Author

Jack Avon is the director and principal consultant at Isys Systems (Ringwood) Ltd., a financial modeling and analysis company in the United Kingdom. He has broad industry experience with integrating in-house systems with Microsoft Excel and Access and developing custom models and management information systems. Mr. Avon has consulted in financial modeling since 1997 and has worked with clients in banking, media, telecommunications, transportation, construction, oil, gas, and the public sector. He is the founder of the Association of Financial Modelers, has a background in finance and IT, and is an avid photographer. Mr. Avon lives in Surrey with his wife and three children.

Acknowledgments

I have been very fortunate to have worked and to continue to work with people from all walks of life and at every level of business; and, no matter where I go, I have found that financial modeling has emerged as a key business tool and that good financial modelers are increasingly being sought after.

Over the years I have made it my mission to get an understanding of the public perceptions surrounding financial modeling and of how people feel modeling can help them. The lasting impression I am getting from this mission is that much of modeling lies in the people. Whichever way one looks at modeling, it's all about the individuals within business. So much about what I know has come from individuals who have given me insights and information, warnings and help, without which my ability to model across several industries would not have been possible.

These people deserve my acknowledgement. Many won't know who they are, but I would specifically like to mention Rob Cotteril, Karen Faulkner, Colin Scragg, and Charles Scragg—all of whom hold a key to why I am here doing what I am doing.

I would like to thank the Apress team including Jeff Olson, Rita Fernando, Stephanie Carino, and Robert Hutchinson for all that they have done with and for me.

I want to thank my wife Jennifer, who continues to put up with my ranting about all things modeling with rapt interest; my eldest son, Luke, who did consider a career in modeling mostly to please his dad but has pursued a career that is more his nature; and my youngest children, Thandiwe and Nathaniel, who are still young enough to believe that financial modeling means their dad is the fastest man in world.

Introduction

This book is written from the perspective of a financial modeler and, even though the concepts may seem rather basic to the seasoned modeler, most of these concepts are the building foundations for any financial modeler.

It has been becoming increasingly evident in recent years that the demands—and therefore the requirements—of the financial modeler have been greatly expanded from the typical spreadsheet jockeys of yesteryear. The playing field has changed, and modelers are now seasoned professionals in their own right and come from areas such as accounting, engineering, and legal.

Modelers are expected to be commercially savvy as well as analytical. In addition, while modeling requires a certain amount of hands-on development, the modern-day financial modeler should also be comfortable with presenting and communicating to all levels of business. Your typical modeler today is not just someone who has a strong command of IT but also has other skills such as project management, change control, financial and commercial acumen, stakeholder management, and communication skills.

Finally, there is a presumption that modelers are highly skilled with Excel (and to some extent Microsoft Access, particularly for data analytics). Though touted as a spreadsheet application, Microsoft Excel is so much more. In the right hands, it's a serious development tool with very powerful analysis features. As the versions of Excel have improved since Excel 2000, it has become a respected development platform in its own right. Applications written using Excel are now often found alongside those written using Visual Basic for Applications (VBA) code, C++, .NET, and so on, as part of many corporations' core suite of business-critical applications. Indeed, Excel is sometimes used for the client end of web-based applications, made particularly easy with Excel XML import/export features.

If I had to select just one key takeaway to impart to financial modelers for your futures, it would be the indispensability of your acquiring the ability to work with and understand your co-workers and the wider public. There is a shift happening such that pure modeling is no longer enough. With all the information you gain from this book, you must realize that all your technical skill will mean very little unless you can combine it with engaging people. Do that and your career in modeling will take you to the higher echelons in a relatively short time.

My hope for you as you read this book is that you acquire an inside understanding of some of the aspects of modeling that will make you come back for more. I also hope that you become more aware of the numerous possibilities of how to model and don't feel restricted to following one methodology. Maybe along the way, as you read this book, you will begin to feel comfortable with starting to call yourself a financial modeler.

Financial Modeling: An Overview

This chapter serves as a background to financial modeling by providing a definition and describing the financial modeling environment.

Financial Modeling: A Definition

Modeling is a specific discipline that often but not exclusively uses spreadsheets. Financial modeling is, in fact, a part of financial analysis and emphasizes the interpretation and output of inputs and variables. A suitable definition should mention processes, variables, and quantitative relations, hence the following definition:

> Financial modeling is a theoretical construction of a project, process, or transaction in a spreadsheet that deals with the identification of key drivers and variables and a set of logical and quantitative relationships between them.

Correlation; measurable

Microsoft Excel as the Modeler's Tool

Financial modeling is very closely linked with the history of spreadsheets, specifically the development of Microsoft Excel. Over time, spreadsheets have become the primary tool for the flexible manipulation of data, and Excel is the dominant spreadsheet tool. Of course, there are a number of other modeling software programs, including Oracle Essbase, MoSes, and SAS Financial Management, that primarily aid in financial analytics. One aspect that almost all these proprietary software programs lack, however, is flexibility. The result has been a boon for Excel, as it has filled the gap due not only to its flexibility but also because of its relatively low learning curve.

The other reason for Excel's success as a modeler's tool is due to the success of the Microsoft Office suite. MS Office is arguably the most dominant and widely used suite of applications in software history. As its dominance has increased, so has the number of applications it offers and the versatility of those applications. For modelers, being able to design and build models in Excel, write Visual Basic for Applications (VBA) code, and integrate the code (VBA macros) into the larger Visual Basic suite to create custom software applications, is a real benefit that is unparalleled. Modelers can also link their models to a data store by using Access, which can be integrated together with SQL server, and then create dynamic, data-driven presentations through PowerPoint. They can then take these PowerPoint presentations and produce automated documentation and user manuals in MS Word all in one place.

Functional spreadsheet applications were first developed in the 1980s with the release of Lotus 1-2-3. Microsoft Excel for Windows was first released in 1987 as Excel 2.0. The very first version was Excel 1.0, which was released in 1985 and was an Apple Mac version only. It was not until the release of Microsoft Excel 95 that spreadsheet applications became widely used within the business world. It was also at this point that financial modeling began to emerge as a bona fide discipline around the world. Since the release of Microsoft Excel 95, spreadsheet application functionality has improved at an exponential rate, providing model developers with the tools to construct increasingly sophisticated models.

Today, modeling is recognized for its ability to enable business decision-making and solve often complex questions about the future. The demand for experienced modelers has risen steadily over time. This trend will continue for some years to come because more and more businesses are realizing that an experienced financial modeler can provide significant added value to any process, business, or project.

In order to meet the increasingly complex demands of model users, financial modelers have significantly improved their modeling skills, not only by being technical modelers but by being experts in business in their own right. Hence, it's quite noticeable that modelers are increasingly coming from professions such as accounting and engineering.

▨ **Note** Excel Versions to Date

Excel 1.0
This version was released by Microsoft in September 1985. This was not a serious modeling tool at this stage and therefore lacked most of the common functionality that we associate with Excel applications today.

Excel 5.0 (Version 5)
This version was released in 1993 and gave us the first look at Visual Basic for Applications (VBA).

Excel 95 (Version 7)
Released in 1995, Excel 95 was a reworked, 32-bit version of Excel 5.0. Although there was little change from previous versions, this version was noticeably more stable and had better integration with the other Microsoft Office applications.

Excel 97 (Version 8)
This version was released in 1997 and was a major upgrade. Significant changes included a full VBA editor with separate code modules, user forms, and class modules. One of the most useful enhancements for VBA programmers was the introduction of Event Procedures. The entire structure of Command Bars (menus and toolbars) was completely changed and enhanced. On the user interface side of Excel, Conditional Formatting and Data Validation were added.

Excel 2000 (Version 9)
Released in 1999, an updated version of the VBA language (VBA6) was introduced, incorporating modeless user forms and some much needed new language functions such as Join and Split. Excel 2000 was the first version to support the COM Add-in model, which allowed users to write add-ins that could work in any Office applications.

Excel 2002 (Version 10)
Released in 2001, there were no substantial changes on the VBA component of excel. On the user interface side, Smart Tags and the Formula Evaluation tool were probably the most prominent additions. The overall appearance of Excel was modified to provide a softer color palette, and the ability to recover corrupt files was substantially improved.

Excel 2003 (Version 11)
This version only had some minor enhancements but did include the introduction of XML.

Excel 2007 (Version 12)

Released in 2007, this version was a major upgrade from the previous version. Similar to other updated Microsoft Office products, Excel 2007 used the new ribbon menu system. This was different from what users were familiar with, but the number of mouse clicks needed to reach a given functionality was generally less. For example, removing grid lines only required two mouse clicks. Most business users would agree that the replacement of the straightforward menu system with the more convoluted ribbon dramatically reduced productivity in the beginning, although this method is now accepted as being more intuitive.

Excel 2010 (Version 14)

Released in 2009, this version featured a few enhancements but was more about making Excel an online application. Excel 2010 was designed to enable working through cloud services. Even with the enablement of cloud services to promote collaborative working, there still remains the central issue that Excel is a single-user environment and therefore cloud has not had the impact that could have been gained were it a multi-user application.

Excel 2013 (Version 15)

This version was released in August 2012 and included minor enhancements, such as the increased smoothness of the user interface and the enhancement of the display of graphics.

Where Are Financial Models Used?

When we talk about financial modeling, we are really looking at quite a range of tasks, including data analysis, scenario analysis, financial management, information processing, software development, and project management. Models are very specific to each situation and will often contain confidential information. As a result, there are very few physical examples of financial models available in the public domain.

Financial models are used in the finance departments of most organizations, but particularly are employed in these areas:

- Investment banking: Risk modeling, option pricing models, and various quantitative models

- Insurance: Insolvency models, actuarial models, risk models (Monte Carlo simulations)

- Retail banking: Funding models (models that can assess client viability by using a number of metrics), credit models

- Corporate finance: Capital budgeting models, cost of capital, financial statement analysis, governance models (SOX compliance testing)

- Governments and institutions: Econometric analysis-based models (used to forecast the socioeconomy in a country or region), macroeconomic models (used to analyze the like effect of government policy decisions on variables such as foreign exchange rates, interest rates, disposable income, and the gross national product)
- Outsourcing and BPO (business process outsourcing): Cost modeling, price and margin models, bid models

There are differing types of financial models, depending on their objectives and goals, such as the following:

- Transactions: Used in acquisitions, divestments
- Investments: Used in capital projects such as procuring new equipment and property development
- Corporate finance: Used to assist in deciding the best capital/corporate structure of a company
- Project financing: Used by banks to show if borrowers will be able to meet repayments and stay within the covenants set by the bank
- Joint venture: Used to calculate returns to various parties at various exit times
- Bids and tenders: Bid models are used to assess the cost of the proposal and to derive the final market price.

The following figures are from a commercial bid model that was designed and built for a large telecommunications organization in order to understand the profits, losses, and cash flows for their outsourcing deals. As such, Figure 1-1 to Figure 1-4 should provide a visual as to what the parts of a specific type of financial model may look like.

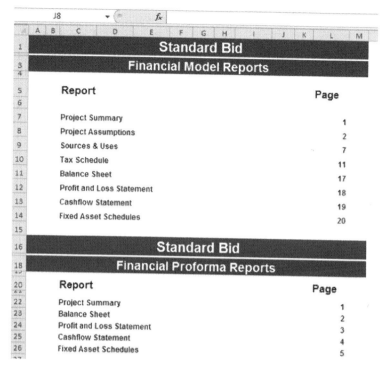

Figure 1-1. This figure shows the cover of a bid model

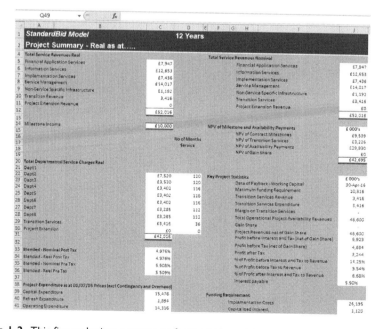

Figure 1-2. This figure depicts a summary from a bid model

| H16 | | fx | 61.0343887900609 | | | | |

	A / B	C	D	E	F	G	H
1	**Standard Bid Model**						
2	Profit and Loss Account						
3	Real as at.....		**Financial Years**				
5							
6		FY (01/04 - 31/03)	01/04/05	01/10/05	01/04/06	01/10/06	01/04/07 0
7		Total	30/09/05	31/03/06	30/09/06	31/03/07	30/09/07 3
8			1	2	3	4	5
9	PROFIT & LOSS ACCOUNT						
10							
11	Turnover						
12	*Availability Payments*						
13	Financial Advisory Services	4,447	.	.	.	.	51
14	Information Services	7,153	.	.	.	.	82
15	Implementation Services	6,436	.	.	.	.	73
16	SSC Services	5,355	.	.	.	.	61
17	Service Management	14,017	.	.	.	.	160
18	Programme Management	1,192	.	.	.	.	14
19	*Milestone payments*						
20	Financial Advisory Services	3,500	.	480	1,449	1,220	258
21	Information Services	5,500	.	565	1,558	505	133
22	Implementation Services	1,000	.	2	7	15	435
23	SSC Services	-	.	.	.	.	.
24	Service Management	-	.	.	.	.	.
25	Programme Management	-	.	.	.	.	.
26	Transition Services Income	3,416	.	362	723	723	703
27	Project Extension	-	.	.	.	.	.
28	Charges to 3rd parties	-	.	.	.	.	.
29	Lease Receipts WIP	-	.	.	.	.	.
31	Total Turnover	52,016	-	1,410	3,737	2,463	1,969
34							
35	Operating Costs						
36	Non-Recurring Pay	5,159	.	737	1,665	1,268	527
37	Non-Recurring Non-Pay	13,103	.	1,578	4,840	2,837	1,862
38	Recurring Pay	11,780	.	35	152	385	562
39	Recurring Non-Pay	8,363	.	75	363	301	224
40	Non-Recurring Pay - Refresh	425	.	.	.	.	.
41	Non-Recurring Non-Pay - Refresh	1,727	.	.	.	.	.
42	Amortisation of Capitalised Interest	1,120	.	.	.	6	19
43	Transition Services Expenditure	3,416	.	362	723	723	703
44	Project Extension	-	.	.	.	.	.
45	Depreciation	-	.	.	.	.	.
46	Lease Rentals	-	.	.	.	.	.
48	Total Operating Costs	45,093	-	2,786	7,743	5,519	3,897

Figure 1-3. This figure is a sample of the profit and loss (income statement) from a bid model

		C	D	E	F	G	H
V89			fx				
Standard Bid Model							
Cash flow							
Real as at.....		Financial Years					
	FY (01/04 - 31/03)	Total	01/04/05 30/09/05	01/10/05 31/03/06	01/04/06 30/09/06	01/10/06 31/03/07	01/04/07 30/09/07
			1	2	3	4	5
CASH FLOW STATEMENT							
Operating Revenue (Turnover)							
Availability Payments							
Financial Advisory Services		4,447	-	-	-	-	51
Information Services		7,153	-	-	-	-	82
Implementation Services		6,436	-	-	-	-	73
SSC Services		5,355	-	-	-	-	61
Service Management		14,017	-	-	-	-	160
Programme Management		1,192	-	-	-	-	14
Milestone payments							
Financial Advisory Services		3,500	-	430	1,449	1,220	258
Information Services		5,500	-	565	1,558	505	133
Implementation Services		1,000	-	2	7	15	435
SSC Services		-	-	-	-	-	-
Service Management		-	-	-	-	-	-
Programme Management		-	-	-	-	-	-
Transition Services		3,416	-	362	723	723	703
Project Extension		-	-	-	-	-	-
Charges to 3rd parties		-	-	-	-	-	-
Lease Receipts		-	-	-	-	-	-
Total Operating Income		52,016	-	1,410	3,737	2,463	1,969
Total operating costs		45,093	-	2,786	7,743	5,519	3,897
Profit before Tax and Interest		6,923	-	(1,377)	(4,006)	(3,056)	(1,928)
add back depreciation & other non-cash items		1,120	-	-	-	6	19
(increase)/decrease in stock		(0)	-	-	-	-	-
(increase)/decrease in debtors							
increase/(decrease) in creditors		0	-	382	172	(212)	(80)
Net Cash Inflows from Operating Activities		8,044	-	(994)	(3,835)	(3,263)	(2,076)

Figure 1-4. A sample cash flow from an bid model

The Role of the Financial Modeler

Financial modelers are primarily responsible for the design and build of the model. They also are expected to manage the financial modeling process—from the start of the project to when the model is delivered and in use. (This process is discussed in greater detail in Chapter 4.)

As mentioned previously, financial modelers come from a number of different professions, but by and large the majority are actually accountants. One of the reasons why the accounting profession is a breeding ground for modelers is that much of financial modeling requires the modeler to have a good grasp of a large host of financial concepts. However, this is by no means the main requirement for being a professional financial modeler. More importantly perhaps is the modeler's ability to quickly assimilate large amounts of information and then filter that information to accurately identify underlying issues.

Ironically, despite the importance of effective data processing in financial modeling, not all modelers are skilled in this regard. In fact, how modelers process and then interpret information is very much dependent upon their experience. For example, modelers who lack business and industry experience will often make fundamental data processing mistakes. If you are a modeler lacking in experience, take heart. Having a profoundly analytical and questioning nature and being able to ask the right people the right questions to fill in your knowledge of a given project will also serve you well. Lastly, modelers should also be comfortable communicating to people of any background and at any level in an organization. When communicating, remember to abide by the three C's: be *clear*, be *concise*, and *cut to the chase*.

Those who do not have a formal accounting background should not let this stop them from considering a career as a modeler. It is certainly an advantage to have an accounting background, but many modelers are not accountants and have found that they are not in any way hindered in their work.

Note Accountants use Excel for financial calculations and to generate financial statements and financial metrics. By and large, these statements are casually called financial models, but this misconception could not be further from the truth. A financial model is not just a series of financial statements. It also involves interactions between variables, relationships of key drivers, presenting scenarios, and looking at aspects like "what if".

Financial Modeling Best Practices

Often clients will commission me to look at their existing financial models and make recommendations as to how the models can be expanded or adapted to accommodate changes in their business. Sometimes I am even asked to completely rebuild a model because it does not fit the purpose for which it was built. In almost all of these models that need rebuilding , the lack of good planning is very apparent—especially once the model's structural features are examined. This chapter will give insight into those features and in doing so will equip you with a layer of knowledge about what makes a good financial model.

What Are the Best Practices of Financial Modeling?

There are a number of financial modeling techniques or methods that have withstood the rigor of time. These modeling techniques that have endured time are recognized as part of modeling best practices. You will often hear the phrase "best practice financial modeling." In fact, if you type this phrase into your web search browser, you will find links to several organizations and white papers on the topic. A more accurate term, however, would be "best practices," because essentially it is a series of methods that each by its own merit constitutes a good way to model.

Therefore, for this book, "best practices" refers to a number of ideals and methods that help with modeling. I generally use the analogy of a chef. While there are several types of chefs and they each have their own distinct style, they all largely prescribe to a similar set of practices and have a similar set of core skills that they adopt when preparing food.

In my experience, the majority of people who use models as end users have never seen a model built to best practices, let alone a fully functional financial model. Why would I make such a bold statement? The reality is that the term "model" is quite general and is used today to describe anything that is performed in Excel. For example, if it's a financial worksheet or workbook, it tends to be termed a "model." The result is that with literally hundreds of millions of financial worksheets out there, a very small portion are out-and-out financial models.

Clear differences exist between a best practice financial model and a general financial model, such as the level of documentation in the model or the ease of usability. When working with clients, I introduce customers to a best practice financial model this way. I open two models for the clients to review, one which is a best practice model and the other is a general model. Then I ask them to identify which one is the best practice model. It does not matter who the customer is, the result is always the same: the best practice model is always chosen correctly. The next section will highlight these fundamental best practices and will also provide examples.

Keep the Constituents Separate

Separating the inputs, calculations, and outputs is a mandatory requirement—this is possibly the single most quoted principle of financial modeling. There are clear reasons for these separations. Separating the modeling stages ensures that the number of errors that otherwise would have been made due to the user's lack of understanding of the model can be cut down.

Separating the inputs and outputs assists with auditing and tracking, which ultimately gives the model credibility as it provides transparency to outputs (the financial statements). The separation is essential and is an indicator that the model has been developed by someone who understands financial modeling. Being able to identify inputs of a spreadsheet is crucial for understanding the effect on the outputs, such as what the outputs are based on.

It is also important that inputs can be used to perform "what if" analysis on outputs. Models lack these separations due to lack of planning, and unfortunately for all who will use them these models are very likely to have any number of acute errors. My colleagues and I at Isys Systems use our benchmark error testing to assess the likelihood of finding serious errors during model audits. Our clients are almost always shocked when we inform them of the frequency and types of errors we have encountered. We find significant errors on at least 98% of all audits that we perform. The main reason for this appalling error rate is that the models have not been planned, designed, and built as financial models, nor have they been built by bona fide financial modelers.

Here is a list of several ways to separate inputs from the calculations and outputs:

- Use different colors. For example, use a yellow cell fill for inputs and a gray cell fill for calculations and outputs. This is usually suitable for very small models.

- Use different areas of a single worksheet. For example, label an area "Inputs" at the top of the worksheet and "Calculations" below the inputs with the outputs below the calculations. This is usually suitable for relatively simple models.

- Use different worksheets for the inputs, calculations, and outputs for medium and large models.

Tip You could create a special style in Excel and apply it to all input cells. This way, you could change the parameters of the style at any time, and it would automatically apply to all relevant cells.

Take a look at the worksheet in Figure 2-1. Notice that there are inputs, calculations, and outputs. How would you know by looking at the worksheet which are inputs, calculations, and outputs?

	A	B	C	D	E	F	G	H	I
1	population breakdown as per Local distributor								
2	Current Population - Length of stay	710			Current Population - Length of stay	506			
3	<1 month	85	12%		<1 month	63	12%		
4	1-3 months	192	27%		1-3 months	96	19%		
5	3-6 months	178	25%		3-6 months	105	21%		
6	6-12 months	156	22%		6-12 months	128	25%		
7	1-2 yrs	85	12%		1-2 yrs	79	16%		
8	2-4 yrs	7	1%		2-4 yrs	35	7%		
9	4yrs +	7	1%		4yrs +	2	0%		
10		710	100%			506	100%		
11	Re-offending within 1 year				48.6%				

	Accommodation	ETE	Tracking	Lifestyle & Associates	Misuse	Alcohol Misuse	Thinking & Behavior	Attitudes
Location1	27.10%	41.10%	31.80%	72.00%	49.50%	14.00%	39.30%	41.10%
Location2	44.20%	61.70%	58.20%	58.80%	35.10%	13.30%	51.10%	47.20%

Location 1

	Needs as identified by SAP data 2010/11	Forecast pathways recipients
Pathways to be provided by ST		
Accommodation	27%	192
E2E (Workshops & Industries plus provision not covered by	41%	292
Relationships (Families?)	32%	226
Attitudes, Thinking & Behavior (Resettlement services only)	80%	571
Finance Benefit and debt	51%	359
Children and Families (includes visitor centre	32%	226

Location 2

	Needs as identified by SAP data 2010/11	Forecast pathways recipients
Accommodation	43%	219
E2E (Workshops & Industries plus provision not covered by	66%	336
Relationships (Families?)	43%	219
Attitudes, Thinking & Behavior (Resettlement services only)	95%	482
Finance Benefit and debt	58%	292
Children and Families (includes visitor centre	43%	219

Figure 2-1. This spreadsheet model design does not separate the inputs, calculations, and outputs

This worksheet would be referred to as model by non-modelers, but it is not a financial model. Why? The lack of organization is the clue, and I will let you in on a secret. The single most important part of any model is not the inputs or calculations but the outputs. Why? Because ultimately the validity of a financial model will always be judged on its ability to produce the output that are required by the clients. In Figure 2-1, it's neither clear which part of the worksheet is the inputs and which part is the outputs. Because of the lack of organization, this worksheet presents numerous questions concerning its credentials as a financial model.

Contrast the spreadsheet in Figure 2-1 with the one shown in Figure 2-2, which shows how the inputs, calculations, and outputs can be separated in one worksheet.

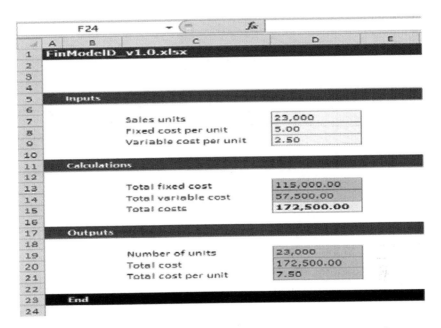

Figure 2-2. This spreadsheet model design separates the inputs, calculations, and outputs

The spreadsheet in Figure 2-2 uses color styles to distinguish between inputs cells and calculations cells. The use of color styles to provide visual cues in models is a recurring theme in models and is part of the modeling styles. Colors give guidance to users as to what actions they are required to take and where for instance using a pale yellow color on a cell is sign that a user input is required in that cell. They also can inform users that a cell has a calculation function and that they should leave it alone. If you intend to follow best practice, use colors to provide visual cues to your users. Also be sure to include a style sheet in the model that defines the significance of the colors.[1]

With larger and more complex models, it is often good practice and more practical to display outputs in a separate worksheet. For instance, you may need to provide a balance sheet, income statement, and statement of cash flows, each on a worksheet of its own.

---

[1]For more about cover style sheets, see Chapter 13 in Jack Avon *The Handbook of Financial Modeling* (Apress, 2013).

Reduce Implicit Assumptions to a Minimum

Sometimes assumptions will get built into the structure of the model. For example, an assumption that the inflation rate of 4% will start from Year 2 could be implicit in having the repayment calculations start from the second time period in the model. Even so, a better way would be to model this assumption with an explicit input so that the user can quickly see how much the inflation rate is in each year and can vary the rate if needed. This would make the formulas more complex, but the model would be more adaptable.

For example, Figure 2-3 clearly shows the inflation rate of 4% in Year 2. Thereafter, it is also stated in each year. In this figure, the inflation has been made explicit and therefore is unlikely to cause confusion to the user. This is an important modeling practice to include because any assumptions that may have an effect on the final outputs of the model will be clear, apparent, and easily read.

	A	B	C	D	E	F
	G1			f_x		
1	FinModelD_v1.0.xlsx					
2						
3	Assumptions & Inputs					
4						
5	(in '000)		Yr1	Yr2	Yr3	Yr4
6	Salary cost		2,000	2,150	2,110	2,205
7	Marketing cost		505	511	510	458
8						
9	Inflation rate %		0.0%	4.0%	4.0%	4.0%
10						
11	Output					
12						
13	(in '000)		Yr1	Yr2	Yr3	Yr4
14	Salary cost		2,000	2,000	2,080	2,163
15	Inflation		0.0%	4.0%	4.0%	4.0%
16	Salary (Nominal cost)		2,000	2,080	2,163	2,250
17						
18	Marketing cost		505	511	510	458
19			0.0%	4.0%	4.0%	4.0%
20	Marketing (Nominal)cost		505	511	510	458
21						
22	END					

Figure 2-3. The inflation rates are explicit and clearly shown in each year in this model

> **Note** Implicit means something is not directly expressed, or rather it is expressed indirectly and is therefore not apparent. Explicit means something is clearly expressed and leaves nothing to conjecture and is therefore clearly defined or formulated. Not all assumptions can be made explicit, so it is important to find a balance between the model's flexibility and complexity. The main principle is that the modeler should always make a conscious decision about whether assumptions should be implicitly or explicitly modeled.

Avoid Using Constants Inside Formulas

It is best to steer clear from using constants inside formulas as they are a cause of major errors in models. You should use constants inside formulas only for very obvious things that never change, such as there being 12 months in a year. Any less straightforward constants usually warrant being separated out just to make clear that they exist. For example, if you are creating a model to analyze the costs within every department in an organization, the number of departments in the organization would be fixed and this would be situation where that number could be used a constant.

> **Tip** Ironically, the way that constants are used in models is an indication as to the competency of the modeler. In general, a seasoned modeler will never place constants within a formula. Test it out for yourself if you have the opportunity to audit or view a financial model. Check for these constants in formulas and see how many you find; a sound model will contain fewer than 10 instances of constants in formula.

In Figure 2-4, the contract duration is 60 months, and a contract end date is needed. One way would be to create a formula based on the constant that there are always either 30 days or 31 days in a month, except for February. The number 30.44 days could be used, but as I later demonstrate, it is far from ideal. In Figure 2-4, the contract end date will be January 1, 2018.

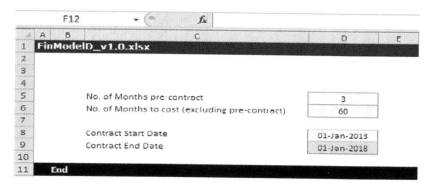

Figure 2-4. A constant has been used in this formula and will now need careful attention

Read through the following formula:

=(D6 * 30.44)+D8, that is 60 Month x 30.44 days + Start Date

The problems associated with using a constant number such as 30.44 days can wreak havoc. Once such a constant has been plugged in, model users must be aware of its use and that it is static. For example, with this model, there will be synchronization issues during a leap year. In addition, in this case, the use of 30.44 days is far too rudimentary. If you multiply this constant number by 12 months, the answer is 365.28 days which if used in models will cause issues with date timings. For an alternative method, see how the contract end date differs in Figure 2-5.

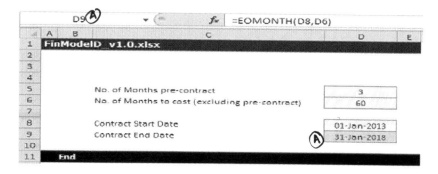

Figure 2-5. A function has been used to avoid placing a constant in the formula

In Figure 2-5, this model uses a built-in Excel function that handles months with the EOMONTH (start date, the number of months after the date formula), as it allows the modeler to use months and days consistently and unambiguously. One of the challenges for a modeler is to find ways of avoiding constants in formula while as the same time keeping the model simple.

Let Inputs Drive Your Models, Not Calculations

The assumptions that you develop for the model should be guided by the final users' thinking. It is very easy to base assumptions purely from the modeler's point of view, which then leads to models that just don't match what the final users expect. This is a frequent and potentially dangerous trap to fall in for many reasons, and it will invariably highlight weaknesses in the modeler's understanding of the subject. Beware of this trap because it verges in the realms of professional negligence. When modeling, all assumptions can be traced and documented to the sponsor of the model.

Tip Consider this scenario. You have been asked to develop a model that calculates staff salary increases every year (indexation). The sponsor of the model has provided you with a salary rate. As a modeler, be sure to use that rate and resist the temptation to create your own rates to save time or to make it easier on yourself. If you do, you put yourself at risk of misrepresentation. If the model is used to make critical business decisions and there is a fundamental issue with the salary rates, you will be able to demonstrate that the rates were supplied by the sponsor and avoid some serious legal challenges.

If there are many different types of assumptions, put them on the assumption's sheet in separate small tables with their own headings. Create groups by using tables and labels for sections and subsections. A good approach is to apply indentation to make the logical hierarchy obvious, or use grouping to separate headings. By modeling in this way, you will ensure that the user's wishes are being considered.

The diagram on assumptions in Figure 2-6 is a snapshot of part of the assumption register from a very complex IT financial model. But notice that for every assumption line, there is a requirement to provide an assumption owner and also a reference. While this may seem like overkill (particularly on a small model), my advice to any financial modeler is to never neglect the assumption register. This is your insurance policy against potential litigation should the assignment get out of your control and go off-course.

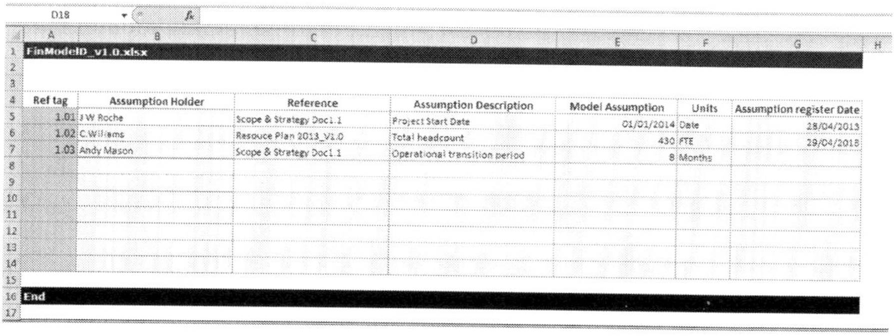

FinModelD_v1.0.xlsx

Ref tag	Assumption Holder	Reference	Assumption Description	Model Assumption	Units	Assumption register Date
1.01	J W Roche	Scope & Strategy Doc1.1	Project Start Date	01/01/2014	Date	28/04/2013
1.02	C.Willams	Resouce Plan 2013_V1.0	Total headcount	430	FTE	29/04/2013
1.03	Andy Mason	Scope & Strategy Doc1.1	Operational transition period	8	Months	

End

Figure 2-6. This is a snapshot of an assumption register. These registers should not be complex, but should who supplied the assumption and give reference where it is used

Have Only One Input for Each Assumption

A very common mistake in models is that of creating multiple input assumptions for the same variable across the model. Duplicating input assumptions will require the user to change a given input in several places. Critically, if the user is unaware of all the changes that are required or forgets to make the changes, then the model will have some flawed inputs, dramatically increasing the risk of error.

The duplication of assumption inputs is common while building large complex models that have multiple modelers. To reduce the possibility of this type of problem, make sure model documentation begins from the design stage and follows through the building and testing stages. Ideally there should be a change control mechanism implemented during the building. If that is not yet possible, consider having a checklist with additions and changes made to the model. When there is more than one modeler, this checklist should be filled out by each modeler daily.

Duplicating assumption inputs is not restricted only to large models. It can also occur when there is a lack of planning on a complex model. I come across this situation regularly during model audits. This occurs because the focus has been on creating calculations prior to understanding the inputs. Then as the complexity of the model becomes greater, the calculations become less adequate to handle the complexity. The modeler will then often lose track of which inputs interact with which calculations and from then on duplication can start to occur. From the model audit aspect, these types of errors are particularly difficult to find. It usually involves a process of elimination to get to the root cause, although fixing the errors is relatively simple.

To avoid the mistake of duplicating assumptions, develop the practice of documenting the assumptions. Instead of just recording where the assumptions came from, also include where it is being used and where it is ending up. This step does mean that the model process will take longer, but the rewards far outweigh the potential heartache of having to recover an assumption input that has complex links.

Figure 2-6 demonstrates a typical assumption register from a model that gives details of where the assumption came from (assumption holder and reference). Take note of the ref tag column. By attaching a unique tag to every assumption, you should then use this tag reference in the model every time that assumption is used. Typically if you leave the first column blank, you can then use this to attach the ref tag. By applying this method, it then becomes quite simple to track where each assumption has ended up and how many times it has been used, which will also expose any duplication of an assumption.

Specify Measurement Units for All Input Assumptions

Model users should be able to understand the measurement unit for every input assumption. These units should be obvious to modelers, but they should not assume that everyone who sees the model over its lifetime will be equally informed. To avoid confusion and especially if a large number of units are involved, designate a separate column for measurement units. This step also helps to avoid errors with the conversion of units. You will be amazed how often measurements are omitted in models and become the cause of confusion. Typically, the measurements can range from anything to currencies, dates, volumes, or resources (usually Full Time Equivalents quoted as FTE).

The Logical Flow of Calculations and Circularity

Formulas should take their parameters from rows above and columns to the left, as this makes the organization of the model more logical. Figure 2-7 illustrates how the model data should reflect how a person can "read" the information as a book, without the need to skip pages and return.

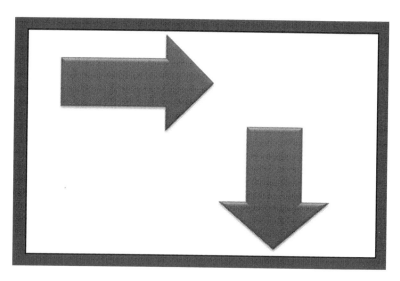

Figure 2-7. Fundamentally, all data must move from left to right and then downward

When the top-down flow cannot be maintained, for example, due to a logical circularity, repeat the relevant rows twice. The ones at the top will refer further down and include the word "circular" in the description. Then the rows at the bottom will be calculated in the usual way from data above and also should have the word "circular." This will make the circularity clear to any user of the model. Nevertheless, always consider if it is possible to use a different approach or to change the input assumptions to avoid circularities, as they usually make models more difficult to use and update. Sometimes, it is preferable to create a macro that would copy and paste values to break the circularity rather than to allow circular references in Excel.

A common area for a logical circularity occurs when calculating interest payments from a calculation, as in Figure 2-8.

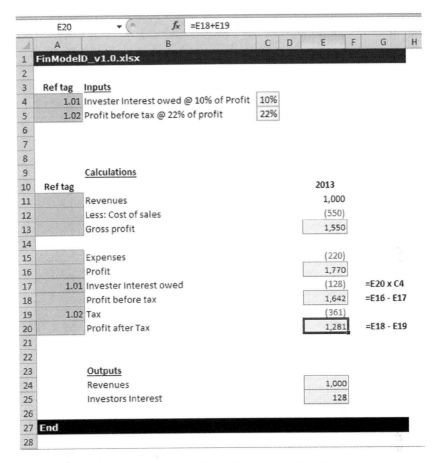

Figure 2-8. To calculate the interest owed, this figure shows that there is circularity on the profit after tax

Figure 2-8 includes a profit statement and what interest must be paid to an investor. The circularity occurs because the interest to the investor is calculated by using the profit after tax (profit after investor interest is paid). You can see that E17 is formula-based on E20 x the investor percentage, which is 10%. As a result, an endless loop is created. There are a number of options on how you can work with circularity, including these two ways:

- Go to Excel Options. In the Formula section, check the Enable iterative calculation option, as in Figure 2-9.

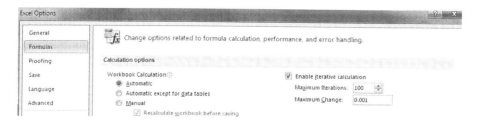

Figure 2-9. Select the option to enable iterative calculations when working with circularity

⊙ Use VBA code (Visual Basic for Applications) to clean out the interest calculation cell every time you enact the code.

Which of these options you choose depends on what is acceptable to your end user. However, consider that it is really a false economy if you choose to enable iterative calculations (the first option). With this option, the circularity will still exist even if you allow iteration in the model. Therein lies the problem. Even though things may appear fine on your workstation, the circularity is likely to kick in again once the model is transferred or opened on a different workstation because the iteration option would not be enabled. When this occurs, it is possible that files could be corrupted and Excel would automatically close down or freeze the screen.

Note I would urge you to avoid circularities at all costs. Not only do they complicate the model, they also help to induce a certain lack of confidence about the ability of the modeler to the end user. As a result, the user's confidence in the model is destroyed. Examine the different ways of working around circularities. The one we most often use at Isys Systems is to create some VBA macro that allows the circularity to be hard-coded out.

Use Consistent Formulas Across Rows

When working with models, it is extremely important to use consistent formulas across the rows. When this principle is not followed, problems and errors will likely occur. For every calculation row, input a single formula and copy it across all the columns. Avoid using a different formula somewhere in the middle of a row. Doing so dramatically increases the risk of error at the development stage and also during any subsequent updates. If inconsistent formulas cannot be avoided, the relevant spreadsheet areas should be clearly marked with color and comments. Even so, such situations indicate a weakness in the model design.

The main concern with inconsistent rows is that users will assume they are consistent. At some point, they will end up trying to copy a formula across or down several cells at one go, thereby overwriting all the unique formulas you have created and plunging the model into generating errors.

Tip Sometimes it will seem impossible to keep this consistency across rows. Once this consistency is broken, however, the model is then vulnerable to errors during its lifetime. These errors will likely end up as the end users' problem. When faced with a dilemma over row or column consistency, ask yourself, "Can I break this into separate columns or rows?" Usually, you can.

In Figure 2-10a and Figure 2-10b, the consistency in row 7 can clearly be seen between column D and column E. But by the time we get to column H in Figure 2-10c, you can see that the formula has subtly changed (the minus "1" on the end is missing). It is no longer the same as the previous columns and has lost its consistency. To compound this problem, there are no visual cues or comments provided to the user to give any warning of this consistency issue.

	D7			f_x	=DATE(YEAR(D6),MONTH(D6)+1,DAY(D6)-1)		
	B	C	D	E	F	G	H
1	FinModelD_v1.0.xlsx						
2							
3							
4	Monthly dates						
5							
6	From		01-Oct-08	01-Nov-08	01-Dec-08	01-Jan-09	01-Feb-09
7	To		31-Oct-08	30-Nov-08	31-Dec-08	31-Jan-09	28-Feb-09
8	Period		1	2	3	4	5
9							
10	END						
11							

Figure 2-10a. In this figure, column D is the starting formula

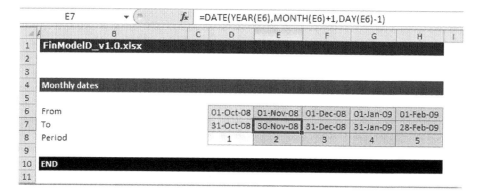

Figure 2-10b. In this figure, the formula in column E is consistent with the formula in column D

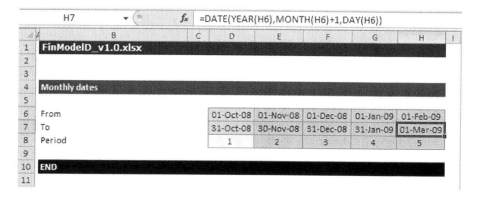

Figure 2-10c. In this figure, the formula in column H is not consistent with previous columns

This situation is not uncommon in financial models and will usually occur because the modeler has chosen to jump straight into creating a formula without considering the design of the model. When performing model reviews or audits, this process is critical to look for and eliminate purely because an inconsistent formula is such a common cause for harm in financial models.

The alternative solutions for dealing with inconsistent formulas all evolve around making the user of the model understand what is happening. From my point of view, avoid inconsistency at all cost. However, if you must break the consistency of the formula, then use colors to highlight the cells where the formula is different (as in Figure 2-10d) and incorporate that into the style sheet (previously shown in Figure 2-2).

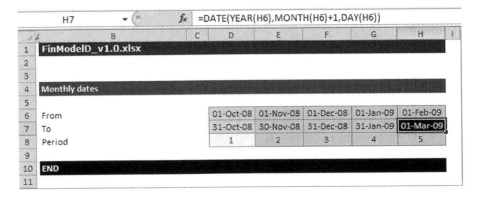

H7			fx	=DATE(YEAR(H6),MONTH(H6)+1,DAY(H6))				
	B		C	D	E	F	G	H	I
1	FinModelD_v1.0.xlsx								
2									
3									
4	Monthly dates								
5									
6	From			01-Oct-08	01-Nov-08	01-Dec-08	01-Jan-09	01-Feb-09
7	To			31-Oct-08	30-Nov-08	31-Dec-08	31-Jan-09	01-Mar-09
8	Period			1	2	3	4	5
9									
10	END								
11									

Figure 2-10d. In this figure, the cell with the inconsistent formula in column H is now clearly highlighted

Avoid Mixing Time Periods of Different Lengths

Often the modeler is required to calculate short-term and long-term projections with different granularity. For example, a requirement might be to produce monthly forecasts for the first two years and yearly projections for a number of years after that. The temptation is sometimes to create monthly columns, followed by yearly columns (see Figure 2-11). Such a design decision should be avoided. You would either need to remember to change formulas in the middle of every row, or you would need to make the formulas very complex to take care of the different period lengths correctly. Both options are likely to lead to problems over the model lifetime because it will become very difficult to create totals without making errors.

J1			fx					
	A	B	C	D	E	F	G	H
1	FinModelD_v1.0.xlsx							
2								
3	Ref tag		Oct-11	Nov-11	Dec-11	2012	2013	2014
4		Profit	120	140	85	1,240	1,320	1,430
5	1.02	Less: Cost of Sales	(45)	(56)	(34)	(745)	(790)	(775)
6		Gross profit	75	84	51	495	530	655
7								
8	END							
9								

Figure 2-11. The mixture of years and months for the dates in this figure will likely create problems for the end users

My recommended approach is to build the entire model using the smallest required granularity (that is, monthly in the case of Figure 2-11). You can always aggregate monthly columns into annual ones on a separate summary sheet. With Excel 2003 or earlier versions, it is impossible to build the entire model on the smallest required granularity due to column number restrictions. Instead, use distinct sheets to model time intervals of different lengths. Fortunately, there are no longer limitations on the number of columns in Excel 2007/10 onwards.

■ **Tip** This date granularity is typical of modeling problems that occur very frequently. If there's any situation that can cause a model to be completely ripped and rebuilt, it is this date situation. Therefore, it is best to figure out how you will overcome dates. If you build your model in months, even if you are reporting in quarters or annually, you can always aggregate up.

Figure 2-12 is an excerpt from a timeline from a back-office operations model. The timeline is a part of the model that acts as a calendar, and it allows users to move dates and times flexibly while still keeping the model base structure. Note that the timeline will always have the smallest date length, in this case months, and then into financial quarters and also years. This format allows the modeler to base the model calculations on months and then extrapolate these to financial quarters and annual periods when required with ease.

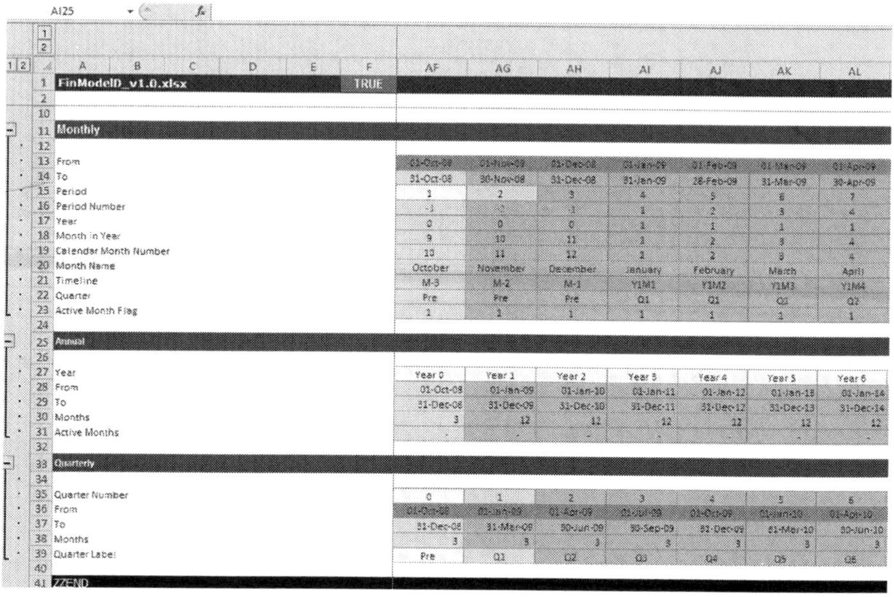

Figure 2-12. This figure depicts the timeline (time intervals) worksheet in a model

Break Up Long Formulas into Simple Pieces

It is best not to reduce the number of cells used by trying to condense too many calculations into a single formula. Writing long and complex formulas that nobody can understand is generally the mark of bad modeling practice.

Try to instead split a complex calculation into smaller pieces and utilize as many rows as required. Usually the more separate calculations you use, the easier it will be to follow and understand the model. With this format, more logical elements will be labeled and the resulting formulas will be much simpler.

Tip If your formula becomes lengthy because you have to repeat some part of it several times, consider creating a defined name for that part. Remember that defined names in Excel can refer not only to cells and ranges, but can also contain formulas. If a formula includes relative references, change it accordingly, depending on where the defined name is used. Defined names refer to a cell or a group of cells that are given a specific name (defined), which then enables the modeler to use that group of cells by referencing the name. They are also called range names.

When creating a formula, keep things as simple as possible; you should spare a thought for the auditor or the person who will use the model. Remember, modeling is not a competition; no one will praise the modeler for having complex formulas, particularly not auditors. The message should be simple and consistent.

Include Automatic Error Checks

A good quality financial model will always have various error traps and checks built into its logic. These help to ensure internal consistency of inputs, calculations, and outputs. Most often such checks represent simple formulas that return zero in case of success and a nonzero value in case of error. For example, to check that a balance sheet balances across all time periods, you should add a row that would subtract total assets from total liabilities. It is a good idea to use different formatting for that row, such as italics or a red font.

Tip Good practice is to provide a consolidation worksheet where all the error checks are catalogued in a dashboard, allowing the user to identify where any errors occur and also the overall model integrity.

Figure 2-13 shows a worksheet in a model. Notice at the top of the sheet the black band with a green cell containing the text "TRUE." By incorporating error checks throughout the model, you can even create sheet-specific checks so that the model user will know if the model is error-free visually just by looking at a worksheet. In comparison, an error would have produced a red cell containing the text "FALSE".

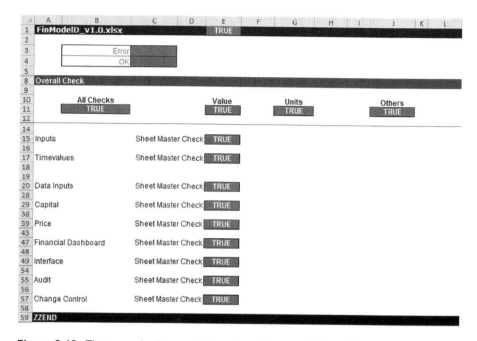

Figure 2-13. The error checking worksheet is used to consolidate all the error checks in the model into one master worksheet

Errors Explained

Errors in spreadsheets are inevitable and therefore should be expected in financial models, rather than dismissed. This section will be devoted to errors, because they are the single most damaging aspect of financial modeling and are so intrinsic to modeling. A modeler who can model without a single error is as rare; in fact I have yet to come across such a modeler. The foremost expert in spreadsheet errors is Professor Ray Panko from the University of Hawaii. He states the following about errors in a paper published in 1988:

> All in all, the research done to date in spreadsheet development presents a very disturbing picture. Every study that has attempted to measure errors, without exception, has found them at rates that would be unacceptable in any organization. These error rates, furthermore, are completely consistent with error rates found in other human activities. With such high cell error rates, most large spreadsheets will have multiple errors, and even relatively small 'scratch pad' spreadsheets will have a significant probability of error.

Despite the evidence, individual developers and organizations appear to be in a state of denial. They do not regularly implement even fairly simple controls to reduce errors, much less such bitter pills as comprehensive code inspection. One corporate officer probably summarized the situation by saying that he agreed with the error rate numbers but felt that comprehensive code inspection is simply impractical. In other words, he was saying that the company should continue to base critical decisions on bad numbers.

A major impediment to implementing adequate disciplines, of course, is that few spreadsheet developers have spreadsheeting in their job descriptions at all, and very few do spreadsheet development as their main task. In addition, because spreadsheet development is so dispersed, the implementation of policies has to be left to individual department managers. While organizations might identify critical spreadsheets and only impose hard disciplines on them, this would still mean that many corporate decisions would continue to be made based on questionable analyses.[2]

You may think that because Ray Panko wrote about errors way back in 1988 things have moved on. While this may be partially right in that we now understand errors, but there has been little change in the number of errors that have entered into models. In fact, this situation has increased as more people rely on Excel spreadsheets.

So, how does all this apply to the financial modeler? Well, we have established that errors will occur. The issue, however, is not that errors occurring, but how they are then treated. Dealing with errors is a fundamental part of financial modeling. The more complex and larger the model, the more likely it is that some of those errors will not be caught. But in order to effectively work with errors, you need to better understand them. This next section will provide you with a more in-depth understanding of errors and why they occur.

The Reasons for Errors

Errors in Excel are seldom a cause for concern in organizations, largely because very few organizations have adequate controls and model review processes. This means that the first instance of an error being caught is when the damage has already been done, which is too late. The reasons why errors occur are numerous, but there are some that are easily identifiable, such as unskilled users, lack of planning, and data and recycling.

---

[2]Panko, 1988, http://panko.shidler.hawaii.edu/ssr/Mypapers/whatknow.htm.

Unskilled Users

Spreadsheet training is not just for new modelers. In fact, lack of adequate training will result in poor or mediocre modeling, such as improper referencing, linking to other workbooks and files, or using inaccurate formulas to master complex calculations.

Focused training in the use of modeling tools that include Excel is one way to help achieve internal control. For instance, long-term learning plans that incorporate spreadsheet training will help ensure that users are up-to-date with the latest version of the spreadsheet in use.

Lack of Planning

If the policies and procedures to mitigate spreadsheet risks are inadequate, errors will become more common and lack of consistency will be a major contributor toward errors not being handled. Therefore, the style, content, and accountability for spreadsheets should be documented in the organization's policies and procedures or in the spreadsheet used.

To this end, documentation is a best practice to explain how spreadsheets are used. Organizations need to explain in common language the purpose of the spreadsheet and intended functions within the workbook file, on the worksheet (for example, at the top of the page), or in written policies and procedures. This way, other users can read the instructions before using it. If documentation is kept separately (such as in a policies and procedures document), it should identify the style and organization-wide requirements for using spreadsheets.

Furthermore, an inventory of spreadsheets used to prepare complex tasks or financial statements will help ensure where adequate documentation is needed. In addition, documentation needs to be kept up-to-date and include who was responsible for preparing or updating the spreadsheet or policy.

Data and Recycling

People are creatures of habit, which is one reason why spreadsheets are reused from year to year. Unfortunately, after cutting and pasting information, the spreadsheet might not work the way it did previously because the formula has been overwritten or a link has been broken.

To help mitigate spreadsheet recycling risks, modelers need to make sure the information added to the spreadsheet is as good as the expected. The following tasks are from a paper by Larry Metz published by the Royal Institute of Auditors in 2008[3]:

- Saving input data separately from the active spreadsheet used for calculations

- Using a control total (that is, a result obtained by subjecting a set of data to an algorithm to check the data at the time the algorithm is applied) to prevent errors in formulas totaling columns of data, numbers, or dollars

- Using self-checks, like a hash or batch total, to verify that formula results are accurate

- Utilizing automated tools to isolate where errors have occurred and could occur

- Making verifications that spreadsheet templates are not changed accidentally by using password protection

Intrusions

Intrusions are the precursors to an error emerging in a spreadsheet. Intrusions include phone calls, chatty coworkers, unscheduled office breaks, or changing work demands. Typical studies, including one by PriceWaterhouseCoopers in early 2000, shows that up to 91% of sophisticated spreadsheets contain errors. The issue is what constitutes an error. In modeling, errors are far more stringent than simple spreadsheet errors. For instance, is a circular reference an error? The answer is that some modelers would consider them to be errors and some don't, and therefore it depends on which camp you want to take. I sit in the camp that circular references are errors because they reflect a procedure that will produce unpredictable and potentially incorrect results.

Who Will Review or Check for Errors?

The obvious answer of who will review or check for errors is the auditor. An auditor's duty is to take reasonable steps to detect situations that may lead to fraud. The landscape has changed dramatically since the days of Enron and will move even further as regulators tackle the case of fraud head-on. For instance, several laws and regulations in Europe and North America (such as the USA

---

[3]http://www.theiia.org/gap/index.cfm?act=GAP.printa&aid=2808.

Patriot Act of 2001, the Foreign Corrupt Practices Act of 1977, the Sarbanes-Oxley Act of 2002, Statement on Auditing Standard No. 99, and Auditing Standard No. 5) have developed an array of regulatory compliance mechanisms, which are meant to deter persons from criminal activities. These laws and regulations have emphasized the importance for the auditor—internal or external—to continually be on the lookout for misstatements that could have been intentional.

There are any numbers of ways to reduce errors in models, but there are positions that should be taken if one is serious about reducing or eliminating errors, such as the following:

- Models of a serious nature should always be accompanied with a model plan. This step gives direction and allows the modeler to create adequate checks while modeling.

- The act of modeling should be left to experienced and trained persons. While it may cost less to use someone with spreadsheets skills and therefore suffice as a modeler, when issues start to arise a modeler is irreplaceable.

- Create a culture where models are reviewed. This can be in the form of peer reviews, model audits, and model testing. Reviews are by far the most potent method of reducing errors in models, as it's unlikely that two people will make the same error in exactly the same place in exactly the same manner. Also there are a number of third party software (Operis OAK, Spreadsheet Detective, or Rainbow Analyst) that can make the act of finding errors a lot slicker.

Real-Life Errors

Whether an organization was large or small, spreadsheets were an overlooked risk by many people until Sarbanes-Oxley mandated spreadsheet controls compliance in Section 404. Flexibility, ease of use, and transferability are a few of the advantages of spreadsheets. However, the same features that make spreadsheets useful can also make them risky.

There are clear examples of where issues with errors in spreadsheets have had an indirect economic impact. Consider the DTF (Department for Transport) in the UK, whose bungled bid of the West Coast train line in 2012 caused a major public sector outsourcing project to make a complete U-turn of the tender process because the financial modeler made an error by failing to add inflation into the ten-year model. The compensation by the UK government to all the potential bidders ran into several tens of millions of pounds.

The experience of the French bank Societe Generale with a rogue trader who lost approximately seven billion dollars through a series of fraudulent transactions should be a warning for anyone who uses spreadsheets to make key decisions about money. This rogue trader managed to conceal his fraud by creating losing trades in European stock index futures with the intention of offsetting his previous gains and was sentenced to three years in prison in May 2014.

It is unlikely that we'll ever know exactly how and what happened. However, a credible theory indicates that inadequate, spreadsheet-based internal controls may have played a part in allowing the trader to build up his positions, which eventually resulted in the tremendous loss for the bank. Some also speculate that, in addition to disguising his trades through a fictitious company and a colleague's accounts, the trader was able to circumvent the bank's internal warning systems by opening and manipulating Excel spreadsheet reports used by managers to monitor traders' activities.

You may wonder how we have moved from looking at errors into fraud. But when you are dealing with very large financial numbers, you will likely be working with financial models and you are never far from the question of fraud arising. As the modeler, you will always be one step away from the model being used maliciously or yourself being connected to misdoings. It is imperative that you always make sure you understand why errors occur, which will allow you to mitigate for when they can occur.

A Tip on Errors

There is a term by Ray Panko that says "keep it simple, stupid," which makes an excellent point: the less complex, the less errors. We need to reduce modeler overload as much as possible. Keeping things simple should also help with reviews and audits. Surprisingly, Panko found that errors were detected much more frequently in short formulas than in long formulas, which may seem at odds.[4]

But note that Panko was looking purely at frequency; the likelihood is that there is a higher prevalence of short formulas over the lengthy ones in most models and hence the frequency will be higher. I maintain, however, that the longer the formula, and hence more complex, the higher the probability of undetected errors creeping into the model.

There is a perception among spreadsheets users that a great number of errors are from mistyping, which does occur. But mistyping is not the dominant cause of errors. Logical errors (such as using the wrong formula) and omissions (such as leaving tax out of the calculation) are also common culprits. We humans can be very inventive when it comes to mistakes.

---

[4](Dr. Raymond R. Panko, "Spreadsheet Errors: What We Know. What We Think We Can Do, July 2000, http://panko.shidler.hawaii.edu/SSR/Mypapers/EUSPRIG_2000.htm).

Catching and Trapping Errors

So errors are going to happen, even to experts, and checking is only partly effective. Should we just give up? Not just yet. We can create methods to either mitigate or trap errors and also create pre-release models (alpha and beta). In my opinion, this is the direction in which financial modeling should be heading, which is going toward a more software development-like process with some sort of product life cycle methodology.

For a glimpse of how error checking will develop for financial models, take a look at the software development life cycle. In particular, consider software and systems that are built but just have no room for failure, such as the critical aircraft system management. One example would be the NASA space shuttle. The space shuttle had its share of fatal quality problems, but its software development passed review. How? Because the shuttle program had put in place so many checks and balances, even with failures or errors occurring, the shuttle engineers were always able to isolate the issue problem and fix it.

On this topic, I would recommend the book *Code Complete* (second edition) by Steve McConnell (Microsoft Press, 2004). While the book is quite technical, it nevertheless will give you a very strong feel of where building financial models could be heading.

Note Industries that depend on absolutely accurate software have very stringent and thorough processes for building, testing, and retesting the software. This method is usually too expensive for most businesses and too much to expect of a humble spreadsheet builder. One thing these industries do well is to build models in small chunks and test each chunk thoroughly. In this way, testing is always manageable. In contrast, when NASA built the space shuttle, they built the main engine all at once because it was at the cutting edge of technology and had nightmares testing it.

The airline industry has to get it right all the time or people die. One key approach is to build in layers. In other words, if one thing goes wrong, another system will cover for it. This is sometimes known as a Swiss cheese security because although there may be many holes, no hole goes all the way through.

The challenge for financial modelers is to develop models that have sufficient error checking built-in that will not just alert the user to the error, but in certain circumstances will revert to a default in order to make sure the model doesn't fail.

▓ **Caution** Be wary of creating models that automatically apply defaults in the event of an error. It then becomes difficult to ascertain where the actual problem stems from unless you design very robust in-model user and system logs.

How to Work with Errors in Models

At the end of the day, we are human and we need to decide how we can work with errors. Even if the errors in the model are totally eradicated, others could easily creep into the model at a later stage. The best way is to create error checking within the model. For example, I build some sort of checks that will alert the user that an error has occurred if it has and will also alert the user that no errors have occurred if they haven't.

Figure 2-14 is an example of a structural error. It is referred to as structural because it breaks the consistency and hence destroys the structure within the model. The sum formula looks innocuous; however, notice the "$" signs. These are called absolute references, and they anchor the formula.

explained on the page

| SYD | | | X ✓ ƒx | =SUM($C$4:$G$4) | | | | |

▲	A	B	C	D	E	F	G	H	I
1	FinModelD_v1.0.xlsx								
2									
3		Sales Rep	Jan	Feb	Mar	Apr	May	Total	
4		John Doe	2,300	1,940	1,866			=SUM(C	
5		Maggie Avery	1,840	-	674				
6		Tom Watts	1,920	2,300	2,005				
7		Agatha May	1,850	2,560	2,211				
8		Tori Smith	1,544	1,520	1,470				
9		Ceri Tuvali	4,020	3,890	3,763				
10		Karina Johns	3,111	-	5,890				
11		Anton Silver	210	370	302				
12		Michela Qunitech	1,153	1,203	1,440				
13		Todd Brown	845	980	744				
14		**Total Month**	**18,793**	**14,763**	**20,365**	-	-	**6,106**	
15									
16	END								
17									

Figure 2-14. *The totals formula has an absolute reference, which will create a structural error*

The problem is if the formula is simply copied down, it will be anchored onto row 4 and will not give the correct totals. In fact, the totals will look just like Figure 2-15.

	SYD	▾	× ✓ fx	=SUM($C$4:$G$4)				
	A	B	C	D	E	F	G	H	I
1	**FinModelD_v1.0.xlsx**							
2								
3		Sales Rep	Jan	Feb	Mar	Apr	May	Total
4		John Doe	2,300	1,940	1,866			6,106
5		Maggie Avery	1,840	-	674			6,106
6		Tom Watts	1,920	2,300	2,005			6,106
7		Agatha May	1,850	2,560	2,211			=SUM(C
8		Tori Smith	1,544	1,520	1,470			6,106
9		Ceri Tuvali	4,020	3,890	3,763			6,106
10		Karina Johns	3,111	-	5,890			6,106
11		Anton Silver	210	370	302			6,106
12		Michela Qunitech	1,153	1,203	1,440			6,106
13		Todd Brown	845	980	744			6,106
14		**Total Month**	**18,793**	**14,763**	**20,365**	-	-	**61,060**
15								
16	END							
17								

Figure 2-15. The formula in column H is copied down but has calculated on row 4

This is a very common issue because initially it does not appear to be an error. However, this is an example of an error being introduced only once data populates the model. For this type of error where totals are being calculated in a column, it is best to keep the formula as it is and avoid any absolute or relative references as in Figure 2-16. (Absolute and relative cell references will be described in Chapter 3.)

SYD			X ✓ fx	=SUM(C7:G7)				
	A	B	C	D	E	F	G	H	I

1	FinModelD_v1.0.xlsx							
2								
3	Sales Rep	Jan	Feb	Mar	Apr	May	Total	
4	John Doe	2,300	1,940	1,866			6,106	
5	Maggie Avery	1,840	-	674			2,514	
6	Tom Watts	1,920	2,300	2,005			6,225	
7	Agatha May	1,850	2,560	2,211			=SUM(C7:	
8	Tori Smith	1,544	1,520	1,470			4,534	
9	Ceri Tuvali	4,020	3,890	3,763			11,673	
10	Karina Johns	3,111	-	5,890			9,001	
11	Anton Silver	210	370	302			882	
12	Michela Qunitech	1,153	1,203	1,440			3,796	
13	Todd Brown	845	980	744			2,569	
14	Total Month	18,793	14,763	20,365	-	-	53,921	
15								
16	END							
17								

Figure 2-16. Totals appear as they are with no absolute or relative cell referencing

Adding Error Checks

While having errors in the model is somewhat expected and we have discussed why, there is absolutely no reason why a modeler should omit building error checking in their models. When I am asked to give assurance on a model by auditing and certifying, it will not matter how well-structured the model is or whether it was designed following best practice if there are no error checking mechanisms. If I don't see any, then that is a model I will not certify.

Figures 2-17a and Figure 2-17b contain a visual error check for the totals by assessing the sum of the total in column H against the sum of the months in row 14, which should always be same. Also in this case, the check shows "TRUE" to signify that the check is correct.

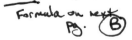
Formula on next pg. (B)

A18			f_x							

	A	B	C	D	E	F	G	H	I	J	K
1	FinModelD_v1.0.xlsx										
2											
3		Sales Rep	Jan	Feb	Mar	Apr	May	Total		error	
4		John Doe	2,300	1,940	1,866			6,106			
5		Maggie Avery	1,840	-	674			2,514			
6		Tom Watts	1,920	2,300	2,005			6,225			
7		Agatha May	1,850	2,560	2,211			6,621			
8		Tori Smith	1,544	1,520	1,470			4,534			
9		Ceri Tuvali	4,020	3,890	3,763			11,673			
10		Karina Johns	3,111	-	5,890			9,001			
11		Anton Silver	210	370	302			882			
12		Michela Qunitech	1,153	1,203	1,440			3,796			
13		Todd Brown	845	980	744			2,569			
14		Total Month	18,793	14,763	20,365	-	-	53,921		TRUE	
15											
16	END										
17											

Figure 2-17a. In this figure, error checking is performed on the totals

SYD			X ✓ f_x	⑮	=IF(SUM($H$4:$H$13)<>SUM($C$14:$G$14),1,0)		

	A	B	C	D	E	F	G	H
1	FinModelD_v1.0.xlsx							
2								
3		Sales Rep	Jan	Feb	Mar	Apr	May	Total
4		John Doe	2,300	1,940	1,866			6,106
5		Maggie Avery	1,840	-	674			2,514
6		Tom Watts	1,920	2,300	2,005			6,225
7		Agatha May	1,850	2,560	2,211			6,621
8		Tori Smith	1,544	1,520	1,470			4,534
9		Ceri Tuvali	4,020	3,890	3,763			11,673
10		Karina Johns	3,111	-	5,890			9,001
11		Anton Silver	210	370	302			882
12		Michela Qunitech	1,153	1,203	1,440			3,796
13		Todd Brown	845	980	744			2,569
14		Total Month	18,793	14,763	20,365	-	-	53,921
15								
16	END							

Figure 2-17b. A formula has been created using a combination of an IF( ) and a SUM( ) statement to create an error check

The modeler can use a creative formula like the one in Figure 2-17b to provide error checks. The model has a built-in mechanism that can then alert the user to problems as in Figure 2-18, where the check has shown that an error has occurred, and will then allow the user to assess the validity of the model outputs. In Figure 2-19 is an alternative method of showing the error check that uses the statement "OK" to show there are no errors. ("Error" would show when an error has occurred.)

A18				f_x						
A	B	C	D	E	F	G	H	I	J	K
1 FinModelD_v1.0.xlsx										
2										
3	Sales Rep	Jan	Feb	Mar	Apr	May	Total		error	
4	John Doe	2,300	1,940	1,866			6,106			
5	Maggie Avery	1,840	-	674			1,840			
6	Tom Watts	1,920	2,300	2,005			6,225			
7	Agatha May	1,850	2,560	2,211			6,621			
8	Tori Smith	1,544	1,520	1,470			4,534			
9	Ceri Tuvali	4,020	3,890	3,763			11,673			
10	Karina Johns	3,111	-	5,890			9,001			
11	Anton Silver	210	370	302			882			
12	Michela Qunitech	1,153	1,203	1,440			3,796			
13	Todd Brown	845	980	744			2,569			
14	Total Month	18,793	14,763	20,365	-	-	53,247	FALSE		
15										
16 END										
17										

Figure 2-18. In this figure, there is problem in the totals formula, and the error check has highlighted the error

| A18 | ▼ | f_x | |

⊿	A	B	C	D	E	F	G	H	I	J	K
1		FinModelD_v1.0.xlsx									
2											
3		Sales Rep	Jan	Feb	Mar	Apr	May	Total		error	
4		John Doe	2,300	1,940	1,866			6,106			
5		Maggie Avery	1,840	-	674			2,514			
6		Tom Watts	1,920	2,300	2,005			6,225			
7		Agatha May	1,850	2,560	2,211			6,621			
8		Tori Smith	1,544	1,520	1,470			4,534			
9		Ceri Tuvali	4,020	3,890	3,763			11,673			
10		Karina Johns	3,111	-	5,890			9,001			
11		Anton Silver	210	370	302			882			
12		Michela Qunitech	1,153	1,203	1,440			3,796			
13		Todd Brown	845	980	744			2,569			
14		Total Month	18,793	14,763	20,365	-	-	53,921		ok	
15											
16	END										
17											

Figure 2-19. A more popular method of showing the error check is by using common language messages

▒ **Note** Error checks are shown in different ways in financial models and much depends on the preference of the modeler. The popular method is to show an actual message which states "ok" when there is no error and "error" when there is an error, as in Figure 2-19. There is no right or wrong, although I would recommend the visual method that uses RED for error, AMBER for warning, and GREEN for no errors. I use this convention in all the models that I design and build because it has major benefits for the end user. By giving a visual cue using the three colors, the modeler will be treading on well-worn ground. This color system is how financial dashboards and project plans are represented, and most senior executives are familiar with the red, amber, and green system. It is also a universal language called "traffic lights."

Secondly, my preference is always to assume that future users of the model may not necessarily have English as their first language. Therefore, I try as much as possible to avoid using English common language messages in favor of something generic.

Best Practices in a Nutshell

Financial modeling best practice is about doing things that make the model simpler and easier to use and also to audit. Here are the essential aspects:

- Keep the inputs, calculations, and outputs in separate sections. In larger and more complex models, keep them in separate worksheets.

- Use consistent formulas across a row.

- Make the formula as simple and small as possible.

- Use styles to guide the user.

- Model timescales at the smallest levels and then work up.

- Do not hard-code numbers into formulas cells.

- Make your layout and formats clear and consistent.

- Deal with errors.

- Always document the model.

- Make sure that you make your assumptions clear and provide references.

Take a look at Figure 2-20. This is an excerpt from an actual model that includes several aspects based on best practice. Can you spot them?

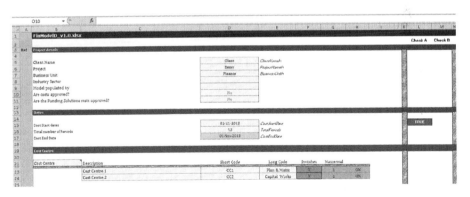

Figure 2-20. This excerpt features some best practice elements

Case Study: Financial Model Gone Awry

In this case study, the brief is as follows:

> *"Deliver a simple financial model that will provide a cash forecast over a period of two years. The model should allow for the user to flex 'what if' scenarios."*

This is quite typical of the information that would be provided for a financial model. Note that as the brief is loose, there is no guidance as to the format or size of the model, nor does it indicate how the output (the cash forecast) should be laid out. The following assumptions will need to be made as well:

- We can assume we know the output formats based on previous models we have built for this customer.

- We know what the key financial drivers are, which we will use when we create "What If" scenarios. The model planning and specification has previously been completed.

This case study will highlight where a model has not achieved the appropriate best practice and then demonstrate how this could have been achieved. Using the brief provided, we will create two scenarios: the first is with a model that has truly gone awry and the second is a best practice version. This case study is from an actual modeling brief, and it is based on a customer who had developed an in-house model that was later rebuilt by a financial modeler. Why the financial modeler had to rebuild the model will hopefully become clear as we work through this case study.

The Non-best Practice Model

The forecast cash flow in Figure 2-21 gives us the output from the model, which we can evaluate.

Figure 2-21. The forecast cash flow output has been determined without any best practice modeling

Outwardly, the forecast output in Figure 2-21 would seem to be intact. In fact, this may suffice as it does provide all that is required under the brief:

- The timescales are correct with the two-year forecast. Additionally, Year 1 has been broken down into the lowest constituent months.

- It would appear that the inputs can be flexed to create "what ifs" by altering the interest, tax, and vat rates.

- We can quickly see where the cash will be at a given time.

- The format is clear, and it is a simple model as required by the brief.

Don't worry too much about the actual calculation methodology. We can just assume this is a given and that all calculations are performing correctly.

The Best Practice Model

Let's turn our attention now to an alternative model in Figures 2-22a–2-22d, which address some known best practice modeling.

Figure 2-22a. This figure shows the results of the inputs

Figure 2-22b. In this figure, the calculations are below the inputs in the same layout

	A	B	C	D	E	F	G	H	I	J	K	L
1	ForecastCashflow_v1.0.xlsm					TRUE						
2	No Such Company											
3			Yr1	Yr1	Yr1	Yr1	Yr1	Yr1	Yr1	Yr1	Yr1	Yr1
4			M1	M2	M3	M4	M5	M6	M7	M8	M9	M10
5			Yr1M1	Yr1M2	Yr1M3	Yr1M4	Yr1M5	Yr1M6	Yr1M7	Yr1M8	Yr1M9	Yr1M10
6			Currency	Currency	Currency	Currency	Currency	Currency	Currency	Currency	Currency	Currency
53	Monthly Forecast											
54			Yr1	Yr1	Yr1	Yr1	Yr1	Yr1	Yr1	Yr1	Yr1	Yr1
55			M1	M2	M3	M4	M5	M6	M7	M8	M9	M10
56			Yr1M1	Yr1M2	Yr1M3	Yr1M4	Yr1M5	Yr1M6	Yr1M7	Yr1M8	Yr1M9	Yr1M10
57	**Cashflow Forecast 2 Years**		Currency	Currency	Currency	Currency	Currency	Currency	Currency	Currency	Currency	Currency
59	Cash balance b/f		-	67,052	125,949	235,453	279,257	325,630	372,322	434,403	496,744	559,345
60	Cash inflows											
61	Core Receipts		£292,639	£292,639	£311,200	£252,199	£252,080	£251,750	£247,690	£247,690	£247,690	£247,690
62	Catering till receipts		-	-	-	-	-	-	-	-	-	-
63	Total cash inflows		£292,639	£292,639	£311,200	£252,199	£252,080	£251,750	£247,690	£247,690	£247,690	£247,690
64												
65	Cash outflows											
66	Staff costs		(£74,167)	(£72,120)	(£65,200)	(£65,200)	(£65,200)	(£65,200)	(£65,200)	(£65,200)	(£65,200)	(£55,200)
67	Materials & subcontractors		(£166,025)	(£155,812)	(£142,001)	(£138,981)	(£137,125)	(£137,001)	(£137,001)	(£137,001)	(£137,001)	(£137,001)
68	Other costs		-	-	-	-	-	-	-	-	-	-
69	ICT		(£2,414)	(£2,414)	(£2,414)	(£2,414)	(£2,414)	(£2,414)	(£2,414)	(£2,414)	(£2,414)	(£2,414)
70	Mobilisation		(£20,056)	(£20,056)	(£20,056)	(£20,056)	(£20,056)	(£20,056)	-	-	-	-
71	Overhead recovery		(£6,517)	(£6,517)	(£6,517)	(£6,517)	(£6,517)	(£6,517)	(£6,517)	(£6,517)	(£6,517)	(£6,517)
72	Total operational cash outflows		(£289,979)	(£256,919)	(£236,138)	(£233,168)	(£231,308)	(£231,188)	(£211,132)	(£211,132)	(£211,132)	(£211,132)
73												
74	Cash movement in period before Int. & Tax		£2,660	£102,773	£200,961	£254,484	£300,029	£346,192	£408,879	£470,961	£533,302	£595,902

Figure 2-22c. In this figure, the monthly outputs are below the calculations

	A	B	C	D	E	F	G	H	I	J	K	L	M	N
1	ForecastCashflow_v1.0.xlsm					TRUE								
2	No Such Company													
3			Yr1	Yr1	Yr1	Yr1	Yr1	Yr1	Yr1	Yr1	Yr1	Yr1	Yr1	Yr1
4			M1	M2	M3	M4	M5	M6	M7	M8	M9	M10	M11	M12
5			Yr1M1	Yr1M2	Yr1M3	Yr1M4	Yr1M5	Yr1M6	Yr1M7	Yr1M8	Yr1M9	Yr1M10	Yr1M11	Yr1M12
6			Currency	Currency	Currency	Currency	Currency	Currency	Currency	Currency	Currency	Currency	Currency	Currency
82	Annual Forecast													
83														Yr1
84														M12
85														Yr1M12
86	**Cashflow Forecast 2 Years**													Currency
87														-
88	Cash balance b/f													
89	Cash inflows													3,138,647
90	Core Receipts													
91	Catering till receipts													
92	Total cash inflows													3,138,647
93														
94	Cash outflows													
95	Staff costs													(798,287)
96	Materials & subcontractors													(1,719,746)
97	Other costs													
98	ICT													(28,973)
99	Mobilisation													(120,335)
100	Overhead recovery													(78,200)
101	Total operational cash outflows													(2,745,541)
102														
103	Cash movement in period before Int. & Tax													393,106

Figure 2-22d. In this figure, the annual outputs follow the monthly, but are in single columns

The inputs are placed at the top of the worksheet, followed by the calculations and then the cash flows. It's important to follow a set rule of how the model will show inputs, calculations, and outputs. Some modelers prefer to have the outputs at the top.

It should be immediately clear from looking at this sequence of figures that there are some differences between the two models, and some are quite glaring. Here is a summary of these differences between the two examples:

- The outputs have been split into inputs, calculations, and outputs, even though they are all on one worksheet.

- The inputs are at the top, and the calculations and outputs run down the worksheet top to bottom as in reading a book.

- There is an error check at the top of the worksheet, which incorporates several error checks within the calculations to give an overall check on the model.

- The inputs are visually marked using styles (yellow cells), and the calculations are marked using green and gray cells.

- The units are clear, in this case shown as currency.

- The calculations follow a consistency. When this consistency is not possible, the color style has been used to signify the change to the user. For example, green cells indicate a primary formula, and gray cells indicate the formula is copied from the cell immediately to the left.

In addition, examine closely Figure 2-23, which features a style sheet to guide the user as to the formats and cell colors.

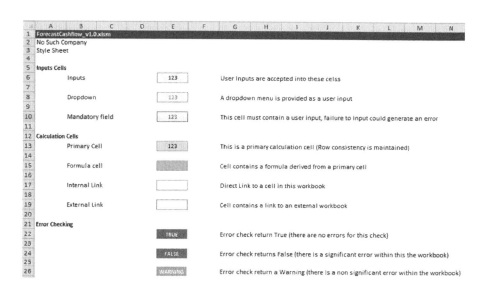

Figure 2-23. This figure is a forecast cash model style sheet

While these models are not the defacto in best practice, they highlight some very simple differences that can be observed from a model that is planned and designed with some best practice with one that is not. Keep in mind that using a best practice approach is not just about looking pretty. There are some major advantages with adopting this method to modeling, and many of the pitfalls that can beset any modeler can be avoided or worked around by choosing to take this approach.

Modeling Functions and Tools

I have been asked often if there is a certain group of Excel functions, routines, and tools that are essential for financial modelers. It's a tricky question because on the one hand, there are certain functions that are a must. But on the other, modeling is a strange beast and very often situations arise that require some thinking outside of the box. When these situations occur, modelers may need to ditch the must-have functions and either create their own or use a totally new function. This versatility is something that separates the good modeler from the exceptional modeler.

In this chapter, I will cover the functions that are of immediate value to modeling. These functions are indispensable and as you build more and more models, the frequency of using these functions will increase. After you become familiar with these must-have functions, you will have confidence to begin experimenting and creating different solutions.

This is a long and technical chapter. You will be introduced to many concepts and skills for modeling. Don't expect to understand these concepts immediately. I recommend that you have a copy of Excel open and work through the examples, take your time, and really become familiar with the functions. You will be using many of these functions and concepts later in the book, so it's important that you begin to develop your skills with using them. Don't be tempted to skip this chapter.

Excel Formulas and Functions for Modelers

This section will include several important functions that are not just useful but in most instances essential for modeling. The notation "Function Name()" refers to an actual function, in addition, where possible there is also a description of the function syntax. I have also provided descriptions on how some of these functions work, which are shown with the syntax. Here is an example: =*SUMIF(C3:C9,E12,D3:D9)* (text will be in italics). Then I have included a description of what each part of the formula is doing.

Most Used Functions

Following are descriptions of some of the functions you will be using most often.

IF()

The IF() function is perhaps the most versatile of functions for Excel. This is the workhorse of functions, and I can't stress its importance enough. When you encounter unusual modeling situations, your knowledge and experience with the IF() function will be a great asset when you need to think out of the box. Those unusual situations will become simpler to tackle.

The IF() function tests to see whether a given condition is true or false. Depending upon the result, different outcomes for the function can be specified.

■ **Note** The IF() function has also been combined with other Excel functions to create such functions as SUMIF(), COUNTIF(), and AVERAGEIF().

If the condition is true, the function will carry out one action. If the condition is false, it will carry out a different action.

The function allows you to specify the actions it should carry out depending on whether the condition is true or not. These actions can include executing a formula, inserting a text statement, or leaving the target cell blank. In Figure 3-1, the objective is to assess the amount of commission on the salary that salespeople will earn once they have reached the threshold of 30,000. This is a classic IF statement situation.

	E4			f_x	=IF(D4>=$B$15,D4*$C$15,D4*$C$14)	

	A	B	C	D	E	F
1	IF()					
2						
3		Name	Age	Salary	Commission	
4		John	24	23,500	0	
5		Mark	28	28,500	0	
6		Rufus	33	29,400	0	
7		Sarah	21	18,900	0	
8		Andy	36	25,040	0	
9		Julia	41	41,200	824	
10		Jitan	22	19,800	0	
11						
12		Commission rates				
13		Threshold	Rate			
14		29,000	0%			
15		30,000	2%			
16						
17	End					

Figure 3-1. In this figure, the IF() statement is used to calculate the commission

Let's take a closer look at the formula:

$$=IF(D4>=\$B\$15,D4*\$C\$15,D4*\$C\$14)$$

If the salary is greater than or equal to 30,000:

$$(=IF(D4>=\$B\$15,D4\$C\$15,D4*\$C\$14)$$ *Bold*

■ **Note** There are two types of cell references: relative and absolute, which behave differently when copied and filled to other cells. By default, all cell references are relative references and change when a formula is copied to another cell. Absolute references, on the other hand, remain constant no matter where they are copied and have a $ character before the column portion of the reference and/or the row portion of the reference, such as $A$5 or $A5 or A$5. The $ anchors the row or column.

Then

The salary × 2%

=IF(D4>=$B$15,**D4*$C$15**,D4*$C$14)

Else

The salary × 0%

=IF(D4>=$B$15,D4*$C$15,**D4*$C$14**)

The IF() function is notoriously difficult to describe because it is specific to each situation.

Tip When you have a situation with more than one outcome, this is where you should use the IF() function.

Use the IF() function with care and sparingly. It's possible to have a situation with more than two potential outcomes, and hence you can have an IF statement with a number of outcomes. These are called nested IFs, which will place many IF statements in one formula. To do this is to show your hand as lazy modeling. Why? This method is untidy and very difficult to track and resolve if there later becomes a problem with the formula. In Figure 3-2, a nested IF statement has been created to find out how members of the sales team are over 40 years old.

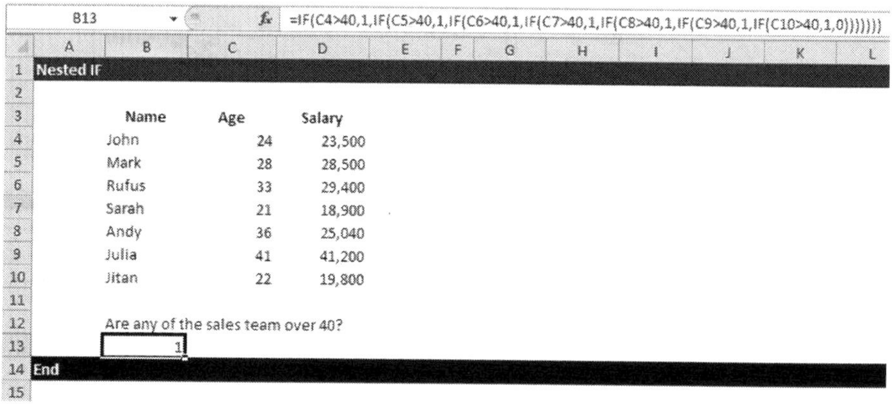

B13 =IF(C4>40,1,IF(C5>40,1,IF(C6>40,1,IF(C7>40,1,IF(C8>40,1,IF(C9>40,1,IF(C10>40,1,0)))))))

Nested IF

Name	Age	Salary
John	24	23,500
Mark	28	28,500
Rufus	33	29,400
Sarah	21	18,900
Andy	36	25,040
Julia	41	41,200
Jitan	22	19,800

Are any of the sales team over 40?

1

End

Figure 3-2. In this figure, a nested IF() statement is used to determine how many of the sales team is over 40

This is a very poor use of the IF() formula, and frankly, this type of formula usage shows a certain failure by the modeler to apply due care and a real lack of imagination. You may be wondering why this is so bad. One reason is that this kind of IF() formula is very prone to referential errors, which can be caused by simple things such as users having deleted a row somewhere they should not have. This type of referential error will wreak havoc in a model because it leaves a trail of broken links through the model. It's almost like having a computer virus; you will need to find the source to correct the problem. Generally, you will find that when presented with several outcomes, it is best to use a table with the criteria and possible outcomes rather than making a lengthy IF statement, as in Figure 3-3.

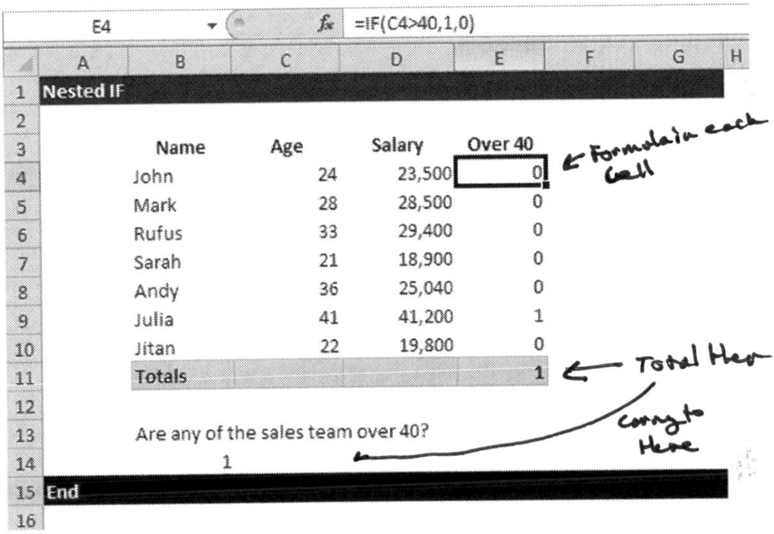

Figure 3-3. A table is used instead of a lengthy nested IF() statement

SUMIF(), COUNTIF(), AVERAGEIF()

There are a group of functions that apply a range of data such as SUMIF(), COUNTIF(), or AVERAGEIF() that meet a specific condition. These are very useful functions, and it is vitally important that you understand how they work and when you would use them. Take a look at Figure 3-4 to see the SUMIF() function in use. Notice how the function will isolate all the data that meets the criteria in cell E13 and will then total that up (cell E16).

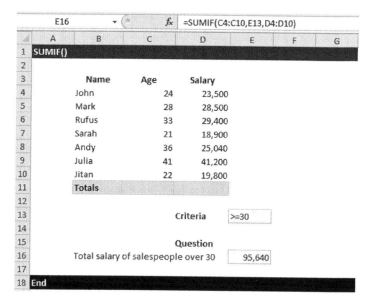

Figure 3-4. In this figure, the SUMIF() statement is in use

▦ **Note** In this chapter, I am assuming that you have used Excel previously to using this book and that you are no stranger to the SUM(), COUNT(), and AVERAGE() formulas. If this is not the case, I would suggest that you invest in a good book on understanding Excel immediately. I would recommend this book for beginners: *Excel Formula and Functions for Dummies*, by Ken Bluttman (3rd edition, John Wiley & Sons, 2013).

Let's break this down and take a closer look at this formula:

=SUMIF(C4:C10,E13,D4:D10)

First, establish the base range that we are testing.

=SUMIF(**C4:C10**,E13,D4:D10)

Then

Establish the criteria we are basing our sum calculation on.

=SUMIF(C4:10,**E13**,D4:D10)

Then

The full range of data to sum

=SUMIF(C4:10,E13,**D4:D10**)

There are many rules with SUMIF() functions. For example, always make sure the base range and the sum range are aligned (that is, they are looking at a similar range). If you don't, you will end up with unpredictable results, as in Figure 3-5.

		TIMEVALUE	▼	✕ ✓ *fx*	=SUMIF(C4:C8,E13,D4:D10)		
	A	B	C	D	E	F
1	SUMIF()						
2							
3		Name	Age	Salary			
4		John	24	23,500			
5		Mark	28	28,500			
6		Rufus	33	29,400			
7		Sarah	21	18,900			
8		Andy	36	25,040			
9		Julia	41	41,200			
10		Jitan	22	19,800			
11		Totals					
12							
13				Criteria	>=30		
14							
15				Question			
16			Total salary of salespeople over 30	=SUMIF(C			
17							
18	End						

Figure 3-5. The SUMIF() formula does not have aligned ranges

Take note that the base range only runs to row eight (C4:C8) but the sum range runs to row ten (D4:D10). This will cause the result to be unpredictable. The problem usually occurs when you use range naming, which was defined before the full data was available, and subsequently more data has been added but the range name has not adjusted accordingly.

The COUNTIF() function works in a similar way to the SUMIF() function. Instead of totaling all the items that match the criteria, this function counts the number of instances in which the criteria is met. In this case, three employees meet the criteria (see Figure 3-6).

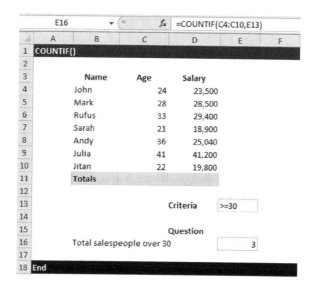

Figure 3-6. Using the COUNTIF() statement, three people meet the criteria

The AVERAGEIF() function works by totaling the items that match the criteria and then dividing that total by the number of instances. In Figure 3-7, there are three employees who match the criteria of being over 30 years old. Their total salary is 95,640, and so the average is 95,640 divided by 3, which is 31,880.

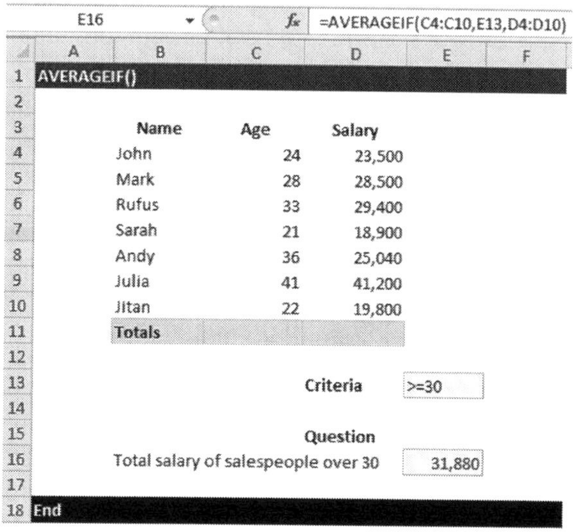

Figure 3-7. The "Total salary of salespeople over 30" in cell E16 is based on the criteria in cell E13

SUMIFS()

The SUMIFS() function came into existence with Excel version 2007, and it's an extension of the SUMIF in that while the SUMIF() only allows for one criterion to be tested, the SUMIFS() function can extend to multiple criteria:

=SUMIFS(sum_range,criteria_range_1,criteria_1,criteria_range_2,criteria_2 and so on).

By giving the ability to work on multiple criteria, the SUMIFS() function allows modelers to create very detailed and flexible outputs, as in Figure 3-8.

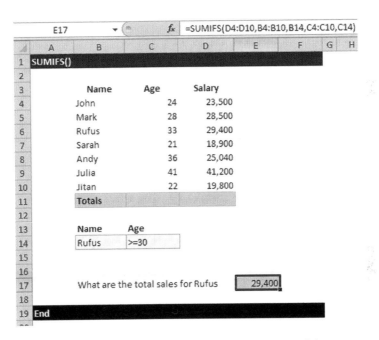

Figure 3-8. The SUMIFS() function is using two criteria—the name and the age—to produce the result

Lookup Functions

Excel lookups know-how is a must-have for the financial modeler. Lookup functions make up a suite of very powerful formulas that can interrogate data tables to isolate items that conform to specific criteria. There are a number of lookup functions, and it's quite common to see two or more of these functions combined into one formula to extend the power of Excel. While I do not advocate creating extended and complex lookup functions because they are difficult to audit, it is still important that a modeler be capable of building lookup formulas that can provide solutions during modeling.

VLOOKUP()

Once you have mastered the VLOOKUP(), your opinion on how useful Excel can be will be enhanced because nothing beats seeing an effective VLOOKUP() at work. VLOOKUPs are a legacy of Lotus 1-2-3, which was the de facto spreadsheet during the 1980s. Here is the syntax:

=VLOOKUP(value, table_array, index_number, [not_exact_match])

- *Value* is the value to search for in the first column of the table_array.

- *Table_array* is two or more columns of data that are sorted in ascending order.

- *Index_number* is the column number in table_array from which the matching value must be returned. The first column is 1.

- *Not_exact_match* is optional. It determines if you are looking for an exact match based on value. Enter FALSE to find an exact match. Enter TRUE to find an approximate match, which means that if an exact match if not found, then the VLOOKUP() function will look for the next largest value that is less than value. If this parameter is omitted, the VLOOKUP() function returns an approximate match.

Note For this book, an array is considered a collection of items. In Excel, those items can be a single row (called a one-dimensional horizontal array), a column (a one-dimensional vertical array), or multiple rows and columns (a two-dimensional array). Excel is not yet capable of allowing three-dimensional array tables.

Excel's VLOOKUP() function, which stands for vertical lookup, can help you find specific information in large data tables or table arrays, such as an inventory list of parts or a sizeable membership contact list. VLOOKUP() will take the lookup value (the item that you are trying to find from the table or list), check the leftmost column of the data that is being referenced, and then work a certain number of columns forward to get the details, as in Figure 3-9a.

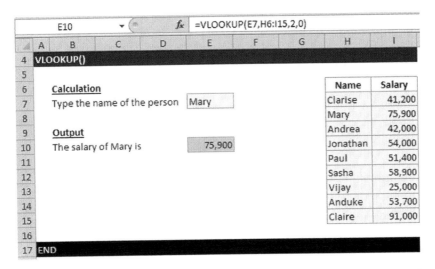

Figure 3-9a. The VLOOKUP() function uses the name to determine the salary, which starts at cell H6

Here is an example of a way to use the VLOOKUP() function. Your objective is to find the salary of the person whose name is in cell E7, which in Figure 3-9a is Mary.

The formula is VLOOKUP(E7,H6:I15,2,0), and it works in the following way:

Look at the name in cell E7, which is Mary.

If the name in E7 is an exact match to any of the names within the range H6:H15, then use the second column in the range H6:I15 to return the salary, which for the name Mary is 75,900.

If the name in E7 has no match within the range H16:I15, then return that it is not applicable (#N/A), which means a formula or a function inside a formula cannot find the referenced data. In essence, there is some data that is missing. If you were to type the name Paul into E7, the result would be 51,400, as in Figure 3-9b.

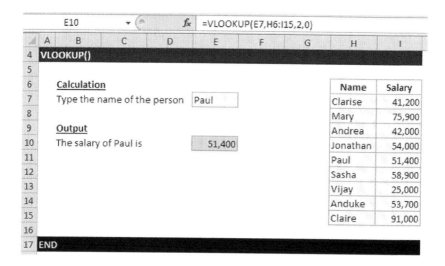

Figure 3-9b. The VLOOKUP() function has reflected the result based on the name Paul

There are several ways in which to use VLOOKUPs by combining them with other functions, which can make them that much more dynamic and versatile. The example in Figure 3-10 is a situation that you will come across in modeling, where dates are used and need to be translated into days of the week. Here I have combined the VLOOKUP() function with the WEEKDAY() function, which gives us the day of the week on which a particular date will fall.

	C5	▾	fx	=VLOOKUP(WEEKDAY(B5,2),$H$4:$I$10,2,0)					
	A	B	C	D	E	F	G	H	I	J
1	VLOOKUP()								
2									
3		Date	Day	Outflow	Inflow	Cumulative Balance		Day ref	Day
4		08/05/2013	Monday	(250.00)		(250.00)		1	Monday
5		09/05/2013	Thursday		720.00	470.00		2	Tuesday
6		10/05/2013	Saturday	(140.00)		330.00		3	Wednesday
7			Saturday			330.00		4	Thursday
8			Saturday			330.00		5	Friday
9			Saturday			330.00		6	Saturday
10			Saturday			330.00		7	Sunday
11			Saturday			330.00			
12			Saturday			330.00			
13			Saturday			330.00			
14			Saturday			330.00			
15			Saturday			330.00			
16			Saturday			330.00			
17			Saturday			330.00			
18			Saturday			330.00			
19									
20	END								

Figure 3-10. The VLOOKUP() function is used with the WEEKDAY() function to give the day of the week

The VLOOKUP() structure is basically the same, except this time instead of referencing a particular cell, I have used the WEEKDAY() function. This function checks the date in column B to produce a number between 1 and 7, matches that number against the table in column H, and then performs a lookup to see which day is linked to that number.

This is an example of expanding VLOOKUP() with functions, and it is a skill you need to become very comfortable with performing. This is the creative element of modeling that you will use to find solutions to problems.

Note that when using VLOOKUPs, moderation is imperative. VLOOKUPs are processor-intensive, and while they are not volatile, they can affect the performance of your computer. Creating several VLOOKUPs that work from large tables (that is, more than 1,000 rows) is just asking for trouble.

Caution Volatile functions are a type of function that will always recalculate. As a result, when Excel needs to calculate any part of the worksheet, cells containing volatile functions will also calculate, irrespective of whether any changes have occurred.

There is some discussion as to which functions are actually volatile and which are nonvolatile, but much depends on which version of Excel you are using. And not surprisingly, there are also degrees of volatility. The most volatile are the RAND(), NOW(), and TODAY() functions. Try to avoid having several of these in your models. Others that are also considered volatile are OFFSET(), CELL(), INDIRECT(), and INFO(), though not to the same degree as the first three. Often the way to get around using volatile is to create your own functions called user-defined functions (UDFs), which are discussed later in the chapter.

VLOOKUPs unfortunately have a built-in weakness—they rely on using the leftmost column for the lookup reference and then counting from that column to find the return data. Look at Figures 3-11 and 3-12.

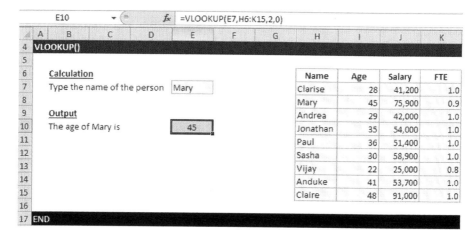

Figure 3-11. The VLOOKUP() function is looking up the age on the correct column

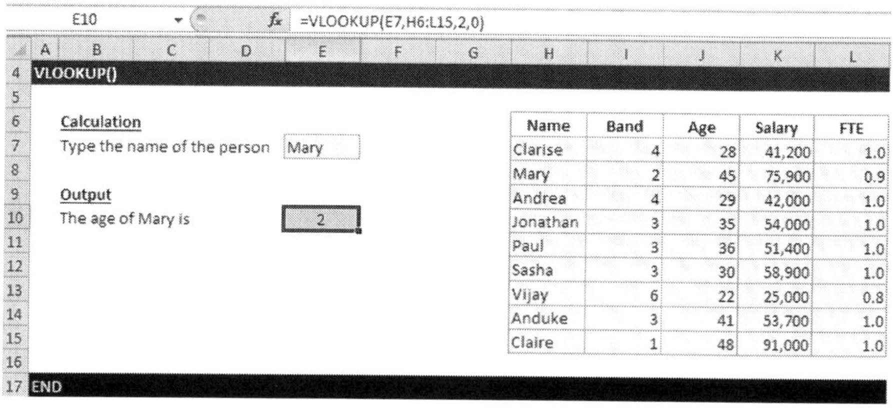

Figure 3-12. The VLOOKUP() function has remained, but a new column in column I has been introduced

From these two examples with Figures 3-11 and 3-12, the only change is that a new column called "Band" was inserted into the table with Figure 3-12. We still require the person's age, but we haven't changed the formula to look at the third column in the table. Therefore, the output is returning the band and not the age. Inserting columns into data is one of the weaknesses of VLOOKUPs. Unless you create some dynamism into the lookup to count off the return column, the model will always be vulnerable should anyone insert or delete columns from tables that are using VLOOKUPs. The alternative to insulating the model against this type of problem is to use the MATCH() function combined with the INDEX() function, which I will discuss shortly.

MATCH()

The MATCH() function can be used to find the position of specified data in a list or a selected range of cells. Here is the syntax for the MATCH() function:

= MATCH (Lookup_value, Lookup_array, Match_type)

- *Lookup_value* (required) is the value that you want to find in the list of data. This argument can be a number, text, logical value, or a cell reference.

- *Lookup_array* (required) is the range of cells being searched.

- *Match_type* includes these three choices: 1, 0, or -1.

- If the match_type = 1 or is omitted, MATCH() finds the largest value that is less than or equal to the Lookup_value. The Lookup_array data must be sorted in ascending order.

- If the match_type = 0, MATCH() finds the first value that is exactly equal to the Lookup_value. The Lookup_array data can be sorted in any order.

- If the match_type = -1, MATCH() finds the smallest value that is greater than or equal to the Lookup_value. The Lookup_array data must be sorted in descending order.

The MATCH() function does exactly as its name implies—it looks to match the data in one range with the data in another. When it finds a match, it provides the position of the matched data.

In Figure 3-13, the objective is to find the relative position of the name in cell E7 (Mary) to the table of names in the range H6:H15.

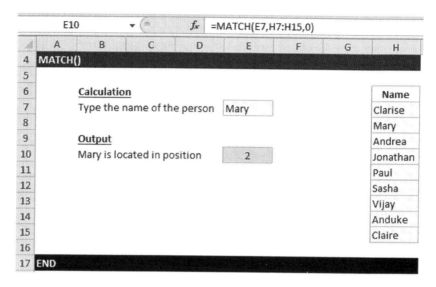

Figure 3-13. This figure shows the MATCH() function in use

The formula that has been constructed is =MATCH(E7,H7:H15,0) (Notice the starting range is at cell H7, not H6 as in the VLOOKUP(). When using a match it's advisable to omit the heading row to avoid confusing the data from the headings.) It works like this:

Hold the name in cell E7 (Mary) and look for an exact match of that name in the range H7:H15.

If an exact match of the name Mary is found in the range H7:H15, then return the position where the match lies in the range and Mary appears at the second position on the list.

If the name in E7 has no match within the range H7:H15, then return that it is not applicable (#N/A!, which means a formula or a function inside a formula cannot find the referenced data).

The MATCH() function is a particular favorite of mine. By just giving the row location of the lookup match, it can be used as part of a dynamic formula that is so critical to most financial models. If you have the ability to reference data in your model by using locations instead, it is then possible to create formulas that can interact with the model user. Look at the example in Figure 3-14. I mentioned earlier some of the weaknesses of the VLOOKUP() function, but in this example I have not only eradicated that weakness, but I have also created a situation where the user can quickly alter the return data. I use this formula construct in several of my user inputs to give the users control over which information they want to view in the outputs.

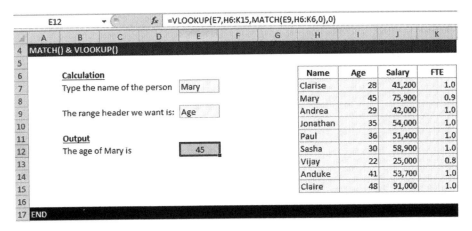

Figure 3-14. The MATCH() and VLOOKUP() functions are combined to add flexibility to the return of the formula

In Figure 3-14, the objective is to match the name in cell E7 to the range in H6:K15 using a VLOOKUP(), but the information we want to be returned could be the age, salary, or the FTE. Flexibility is a must.

For this situation, I used a combination of a VLOOKUP() and a MATCH() function because no single function is able to give the flexibility around the data. The formula construction is: =VLOOKUP(E7,H6:K15,MATCH(E9,H6:K6,0),0). This is how it works:

Hold the name in cell E7 (Mary) and look for an exact match of that name within the range H6:K15.

The second half of the formula uses the MATCH() function to find the relative column location of "Age" in the table, which is column 2.

The whole formula is then looking up the name Mary in the table, and then finding the heading column two which is the age, and then returning the value of Mary's age.

If the name Mary in E7 and/or the range header in E9 have no match within the range H6:K15, return that it is not applicable (#N/A!).

One of the benefits of using this formula construction is that there is stability with data because the matching is using references in the range. Notice that in Figure 3-15a I have inserted a new column called "Band" into column I; this has altered the range structure as it has changed from a four-column range to a five-column range. A common problem with lookups is creating a formula that uses a number as the column reference that will provide the return information. If we look at Figure 3-15b, the MATCH() function has been exchanged for a numerical reference to the return column and the result is the same. However, in Figure 3-15c, the result has become unpredictable because the range structure has been changed and a new column inserted.

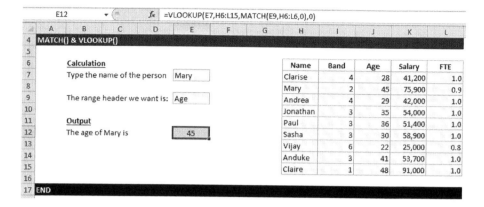

Figure 3-15a. The formula still remains the same and returns the same results even with a new column inserted called "Band"

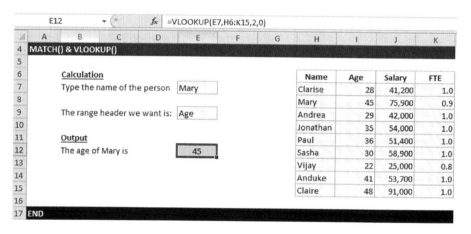

Figure 3-15b. The MATCH() function has been replaced with a numerical reference to the column (2) in the formula, and Mary's age is matched correctly

E12				f_x	=VLOOKUP(E7,H6:L15,2,0)					
A	B	C	D	E	F	G	H	I	J	K	L

4	MATCH() & VLOOKUP()						
5							
6	Calculation				Name	Band	Age	Salary	FTE
7	Type the name of the person	Mary			Clarise	4	28	41,200	1.0
8					Mary	2	45	75,900	0.9
9	The range header we want is:	Age			Andrea	4	29	42,000	1.0
10					Jonathan	3	35	54,000	1.0
11	Output				Paul	3	36	51,400	1.0
12	The age of Mary is		2		Sasha	3	30	58,900	1.0
13					Vijay	6	22	25,000	0.8
14					Anduke	3	41	53,700	1.0
15					Claire	1	48	91,000	1.0
16								
17	END						

Figure 3-15c. The range structure has been changed and a new column has been added. As a result, the use of a numerical column reference has caused the results to become unpredictable

INDEX()

The INDEX() function is a two-horse cart; it can either return the value from a table or return the location reference within a table. Here is the syntax for when a value needs to be returned:

INDEX(array, row_number, [column_number])

- *Array* is a range of cells or table.

- *Row_number* is the row number in the array to use to return the value. If this value is omitted, then the Column_ number is required.

- *Column_number* is optional. It is the column number in the array to use to return the value. If this number is omitted, then the Row_number is required.

Figure 3-16 demonstrates using the INDEX() function to return a value. The objective is to see which value is returned based on a specified location within a table.

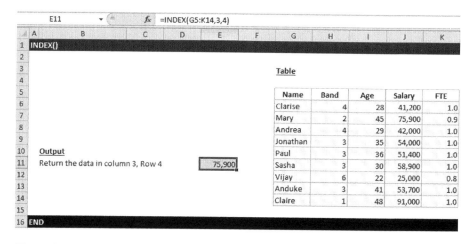

Figure 3-16. The INDEX() function is used to return the value found by referencing the rows and columns

For this situation, I used the INDEX() function with the formula =INDEX(G5:K14,3,4). Here is how it works:

Take the range of cells from G5:K14 Starting from the first cell (G5), move down three cell rows (including G5), and then move across four cell columns (including G5), which returns 75,900.

If the locations of rows and columns are not within the table, then return #REF!, which means the reference is invalid.

This is quite a simple formula to construct using the table and stating the row and column numbers. The INDEX() function together with the MATCH() function is also an effective alternative to using VLOOKUPs, and there are numerous reasons why. The main one is that such a formula does not rely on the leftmost column to read the data. Therefore, the formula can be used to work backward from a table as well as forward. The combination also has benefits by using it dynamically, as in Figure 3-17.

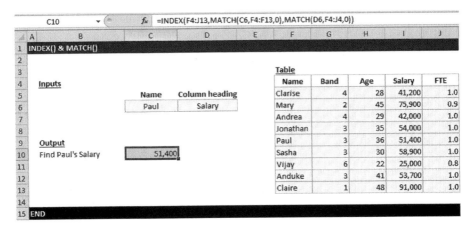

Figure 3-17. In this figure, the INDEX() and MATCH() functions are used in cell C10

In Figure 3-17, the objective is to find the value that satisfies two criteria—the name and a flexible column heading (in this case it is the salary).

For this situation, I used a combination of the INDEX() and MATCH() functions with the formula:

=INDEX(F4:J13,MATCH(C6,F4:F13,0),MATCH(D6,F4:J4,0))

Here is how it works:

Take the range of cells from F4:J13 and then find the name in cell C6 within the table F4:J13. Then using the same row of the name in C6, move across the columns until you get to the heading in cell D6 (Salary) and return the value that is in that cell.

If neither the name or column headings match the table, then return #N/A!

Using the combination of the INDEX() and MATCH() functions is also a way of giving the user inputs flexibility. When designing financial models, it is critical to give as much flexibility as you can afford to the model user. These types of formula constructs will aid you in offering this flexibility.

OFFSET()

The syntax for the OFFSET() function is as follows:

=OFFSET(starting_point, rows to move, columns to move, height, width)

The OFFSET() function returns a cell or range of cells that is a specified number of rows and columns from the original cell or range of cells (see Figure 3-18a).

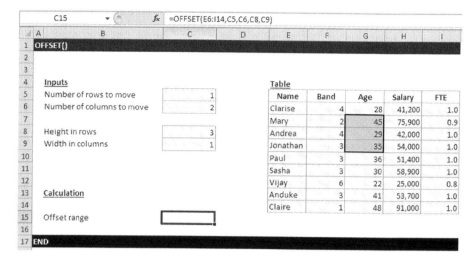

Figure 3-18a. This figure shows the OFFSET() function acting on a set of data

Let's break this formula down in order to examine it more closely:

$$=OFFSET(E6:I14,C5,C6,C8,C9)$$

Take the range from cells E6 to I14 as the reference.

$$=\mathbf{OFFSET(E6:I14},C5,C6,C8,C9)$$

Then move the specified number of rows across starting from cell E6 as input in cell C5 (in this case one row).

$$=OFFSET(\mathbf{E6}:I14,\mathbf{C5},C6,C8,C9)$$

Then move the specified number of columns across starting from cell E6 as input in cell C6 (in this case two columns).

$$=OFFSET(\mathbf{E6}:I14,C5,\mathbf{C6},C8,C9)$$

The range to cover is now based on cell C8 in rows (in this case three) and cell C9 in columns (in this case one).

$$=OFFSET(\mathbf{E6}:I14,C5,C6,\mathbf{C8,C9})$$

The range that is the offset range is marked in blue in Figure 3-18a. The OFFSET() function is not used frequently in modeling, because it is not immediately clear what to use it for, and also because it is one of the few functions that, when used on its own, does not give a valid return. In fact the OFFESET() is almost always used with in conjunction with the SUM() function, COUNT() function, and sometimes with the MATCH() function. However, the OFFSET() function should not be overlooked because there are situations where it is useful. For example, it would be needed if the model is expecting to have some data inputs from the model user into a table. In Figure 3-18b, I have shown a simple example of using the SUM() function to total the cells from the OFFSET() function.

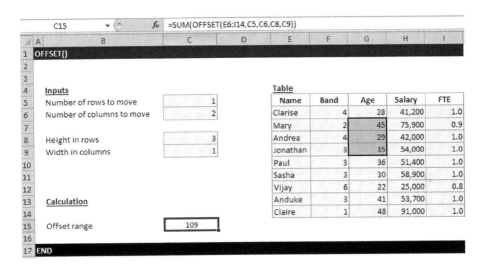

| C15 | | f_x | =SUM(OFFSET(E6:I14,C5,C6,C8,C9)) | | | | | | |

A	B	C	D	E	F	G	H	I
1 OFFSET()								
4	Inputs			Table				
5	Number of rows to move	1		Name	Band	Age	Salary	FTE
6	Number of columns to move	2		Clarise	4	28	41,200	1.0
7				Mary	2	45	75,900	0.9
8	Height in rows	3		Andrea	4	29	42,000	1.0
9	Width in columns	1		Jonathan	3	35	54,000	1.0
10				Paul	3	36	51,400	1.0
11				Sasha	3	30	58,900	1.0
12				Vijay	6	22	25,000	0.8
13	Calculation			Anduke	3	41	53,700	1.0
14				Claire	1	48	91,000	1.0
15	Offset range	109						
17 END								

Figure 3-18b. The OFFSET() function has highlighted the data based on the inputs. These inputs are then totaled by using the SUM() function

Caution The OFFSET() function is often volatile, which I explained earlier in this chapter. Therefore you should limit the number of times that it is used in your model. As a general rule, have no more than one OFFSET() function on any given worksheet.

CHOOSE()

The CHOOSE() function is used when there is a need to choose between a number of options. Even though it is not often used in modeling, it is a simple and very useful function that I would advise you to put into your modeling tools armory. The syntax is as follows:

=CHOOSE(index_num, value1, value2, value3 ... up to 254 values)

The example in Figure 3-19 shows the practical use of the CHOOSE() function when choosing from a set of options.

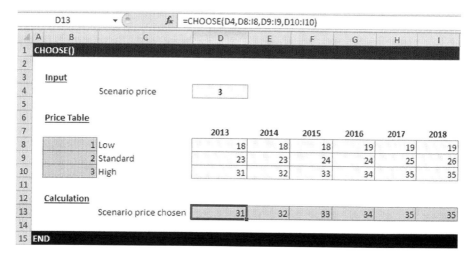

Figure 3-19. In this figure, the CHOOSE() function is used when picking out one option

In Figure 3-19, there is a table with three pricing options (low, standard, and high), numbered 1, 2, 3 respectively. There is a scenario price option in cell D4, which allows the model user to choose one of the three numbers (1, 2, or 3)

Once the user has selected one of the numbers, a CHOOSE() function will then return the data that corresponds to that number. Let's take a closer look at this function.

First use the index number in cell D4.

=CHOOSE(D4,*D8:I8:D9:I9:D10:I10).*

Then use reference number 1 from cell D8 to I8, reference number 2 from cell D9 to I9, and reference number 3 from cell D10 to I10. Then match the reference number to the index number chosen and display the relevant price.

*=CHOOSE(C6,D9:***K9,D10:K10,D1:K11***)*

The example in Figure 3-19 is a very common occurrence in models where you need to show distinct viewpoints or when you need to reflect many unlike scenarios from a set of data. Becoming familiar with the working of the CHOOSE() function will provide you with a relatively easy solution to modeling scenarios.

Date and Time Functions

Dates are very important in financial modeling because they just crop up time and time again. Almost all the information that is produced as outputs have a time impact; therefore, at some juncture in every model dates have to be dealt with. My advice to you is to come to grips with working with dates. Many users of Excel find dates tricky because dates do not conform to the binary formats. But with a little perseverance, you will overcome any inhibitions you have concerning dates, and it will be worth it to you.

NETWORKDAYS.INTL()

The NETWORKDAYS.INTL() function is used to calculate the number of whole business or working days between the start date and end date that is specified in the formula. You may have come across the NETWORKDAYS() function previously, but the NETWORKDAYS.INTL() function is different. This function allows you to specify which days and how many are considered weekend days rather than automatically removing two days per week (such as removing Saturday and Sunday from the total number of days), which is more practical.

With this function, days specified as weekend days are automatically removed from the total. In addition, specific days, such as statutory holidays, can be omitted as well, all within the formula in contrast to making adjustments if you use NETWORKDAYS().

The syntax for the NETWORKDAYS.INTL() function is as follows:

= NETWORKDAYS.INTL(Start_date, End_date, Weekend, Holidays)

- *Start_date* (required) is the start date of the chosen time period. This function does not have real time date valida-tion (avoid entering dates directly into the formula), and so you should always use a cell reference that is expect-ing a date to avoid issues related to date syntax.

- *End_date* (required) is the end date of the chosen time period. As with the Start_date, use a cell reference that is expecting a date.

- *Weekend* (optional) is the number of days and which days of the week with 1 = Saturday and Sunday, 6 = Thursday and Friday, and 7 = Friday and Saturday. If this weekend option is left blank, then the function will revert to the default, which is number 1 (Saturday and Sunday).

- *Holidays* (optional) are more additional dates (sometimes it is just one date) that are excluded from the full number of working days. Although it is possible to enter the series of holidays as dates, I advise that you use a reference to a range that contains the holiday dates. If you don't, the formula construction becomes cumbersome (see Figure 3-20).

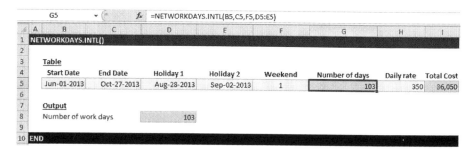

Figure 3-20. Calculating the number of working days is served by using the NETWORKDAYS.INTL() function

DATEDIF()

The DATEDIF() function is used to calculate the time period or difference between two dates. This time period can be calculated as the number of days, months, or years between the two dates. You will often find that you will need to make some modeling calculation based on a time lapse. The function is very useful when a certain passage of time has elapsed that will trigger some mechanism.

An interesting point about DATEDIF() is that it is an "undocumented" function. This means that it is not listed with other date functions under the Formula tab in Excel, so you won't find it if you try to look for it in the Formula dialog. Therefore, you will need to type it in manually and not rely on the formula defaults.

The syntax for the DATEDIF() function is as follows:

=DATEDIF(start_date,end_date, "interval")

The function has three arguments that need to be entered as part of the function:

- *Start_date* (required) is the start date of the chosen time period. This function does not have real time date validation, and so you should always use a cell reference to the start date to avoid date syntax issues.

- *End_date* (required) is the end date of the chosen time period. As with the Start_date, use a cell reference for the end_date.

- *"Interval"* (required) tells the function to find the number of days ("D"), complete months ("M"), or complete years ("Y") between the two dates.

Caution When entering the interval argument, you must include the quotation marks such as "YD." Always remember there is a space before the quotation marks.

The interval argument can also contain a combination of days, months, and years in order to increase the variety of answers returned by the function.

- "YM" calculates the number of months between two dates as if the dates were in the same year.

- "YD" calculates the number of days between two dates as if the dates were in the same year.

- "MD" calculates the number of days between two dates as if the dates were in the same month and year.

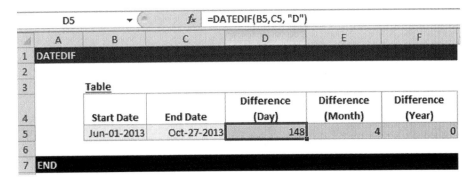

	A	B	C	D	E	F
			D5	f_x =DATEDIF(B5,C5, "D")		
1	DATEDIF					
2						
3		Table				
4		Start Date	End Date	Difference (Day)	Difference (Month)	Difference (Year)
5		Jun-01-2013	Oct-27-2013	148	4	0
6						
7	END					

Figure 3-21a. This figure shows the DATEDIF() function using the day ("D")

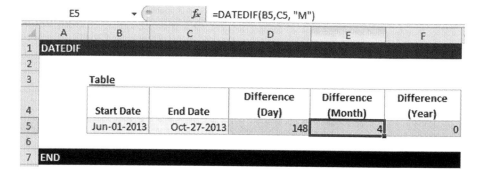

Figure 3-21b. This figure shows the DATEDIF() function using the month ("M")

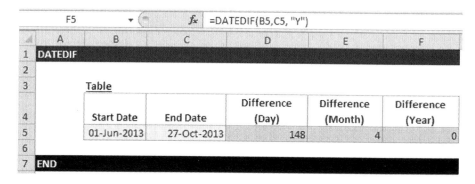

Figure 3-21c. This figure shows the DATEDIF() function using the year ("Y")

As the DATEDIF() function has to be typed manually, it is very easy to mistype it as DATEIF() and then receive a naming error. This can be quite frustrating, but just remember there is a "D" after the "DATE".

WORKDAY()

The WORKDAY() function finds the start or end date of a project or assignment. This is another workhorse function—you will use it time and time again. One of the real benefits of this function is that it can be used to check the user inputs and then calculate number of days thereafter. I use this function in tax calculations and also where there are schedules, such as amortization and depreciation calculations.

The number of workdays automatically excludes weekends and any dates that are identified as holidays.

Uses for the WORKDAY() function include calculating the following:

- The end date for a project with a set number of workdays following a given start date
- The start date for a project with a set number of workdays before a given end date
- The due date for an invoice
- The expected delivery date for goods or materials

The syntax for the WORKDAY() function is as follows:

$$=WORKDAY(Start\_date, Days, Holidays)$$

- *Start_date* (required) is the start date of the chosen time period. The actual start date can be entered for this argument or the cell reference to the location of this data in the worksheet can be entered instead.

- *Days* (required) is the length of the project. This is an integer showing the number of days of work that were performed on the project. For this argument, enter the number of days of work or the cell reference to the location of this data in the worksheet.

- *Holidays* (optional) is one or more additional dates that are not counted as part of the total number of working days. Use the cell reference to the location of the data in the worksheet for this argument.

Note To find a date that occurs after the Start_date argument, use a positive integer for Days. To find a date that occurs before the Start_date argument, use a negative integer for Days. In this second situation, the Start_date argument could be identified as the end date of a project.

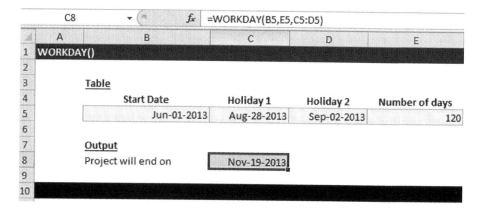

Figure 3-22. The WORKDAY() function also using the optional holidays and the start date to produce an end date

Let's look at this formula more closely:

First get the start date.

$$=WORKDAY(B5,E5,C5:D5)$$

Then get the number of days projected.

$$=WORKDAY(B4,\mathbf{E5},C5:D5)$$

Next, add the start date and end date of the holidays (optional).

$$=WORKDAY(B5,E5,\mathbf{C5:D5})$$

■ **Caution** Be wary of how you use the holiday options. If you do use them, the formula actually adds the holidays to the total number of days. In reality, most projects or work processes do not work in this way. Holidays are incidental and do not get added onto projects because they are already built around the number of days. As a result, you could be double-counting. If you are not sure, just reduce the number of days by the number of holidays.

EOMONTH()

The EOMONTH() function (or End of Month function) defaults to the end-of-month date for any start date and the number of months before or after that date between -12 to 12.

Here is the syntax for the EOMONTH() function:

$$= EOMONTH(Start\_date, Months)$$

- *Start_date* is the start date of the project or time period in question.

- *Months* is the number of months before or after the Start_date.

It may seem curious looking at this function as to when you would ever use it. Surprisingly, the EOMONTH() is a very commonly used function in financial models. It is most useful when you need to set time scales based on a flexible date. For instance, I use this function in outsourcing bid models to check when the model user's project start date begins. I would then set a preproject bid preparation period that is based on this start date, as in Figure 3-23.

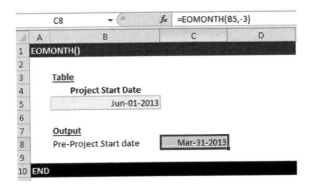

Figure 3-23. The EOMONTH() function is used to set the preproject date

---

Note Keep in mind that the EOMONTH() function will always give the end of the month irrespective of the start date.

DAYS360()

The DAYS360 function gives the number of days between two dates, but it is based on a 360 days per annum in contrast to the full calendar year. I am not sure why this function is based on a 360-day year, but it just means the modeler should be aware that the function is out of synchronization with the calendar year. However, this is an important function when trying to create payment terms or creditor and debtor terms in your models as every month is 30 days (it's quite common for organizations to have payment terms that are built on 30 days, 60 days, or even 90 days).

Here is the syntax for the DAYS360() function:

$$= DAYS360(Start\_date, End\_date, Method\,)$$

- *Start_date* is the start date of the chosen time period.
- *End_date* is the end date of the chosen time period.
- *Method* is a Boolean value (TRUE or FALSE).
- *If FALSE* uses the US method of calculating start and end dates.
- *If TRUE* uses the European method of calculating start and end dates.

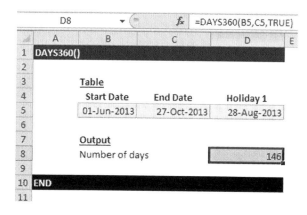

Figure 3-24. The DAYS360() function is shown in this figure

DATE()

I have previously mentioned that dates are often one of the key drivers in financial models. Excel treats dates as numbers and, although these numbers can be formatted to represent months, days, and years, they are still essentially a number. Excel generally recognizes dates when they are simply typed in, such as 06/21/2013. However, depending on how the cell has been formatted, that date could actually be a text (as opposed to a numeric), in which case it will not be recognized.

When working with these functions, I recommend that you use the DATE() function rather than simply typing dates as in Figure 3-25. This function will clarify the numeric date irrespective of the cell format.

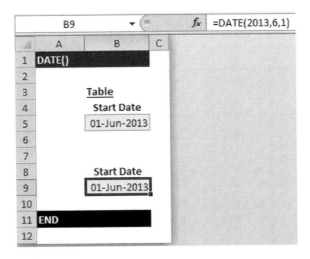

Figure 3-25. The date in row 5 is manually typed, and the date in row 9 is using the DATE() function

The syntax for the DATE() function is as follows:

$$= DATE(Year, Month, Day)$$

- *Year*: Enter the year as a four-digit number or the cell reference where it is located.

- *Month*: Enter the year as a two-digit number or the cell reference where it is located.

- *Day*: Enter the day as a two-digit number or the cell reference where it is located.

Math Functions

Math functions are a used to calculate particular mathematical problems and, while these functions are in common use, such as the SUM() function, they need to be treated with care because they give specific returns.

MOD()

The MOD() function is used to divide numbers. But unlike a regular division, it returns the remainder as the answer.

The syntax for the MOD() function is as follows:

$$= MOD(Number, Divisor)$$

This function is particularly useful when trying to set events or triggers within a model that occur at regular and irregular time intervals and could also then trigger some action. In Figure 3-26, the objective is to set a trigger that will allow us to identify when a bill should be sent based on the month. The formula is =MOD(E10,$D$5). Let's see how it works.

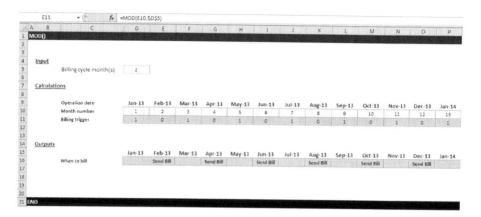

Figure 3-26. The MOD() function is used to return the divisor set by the billing

Take the month number starting from cell D10 to P10 and divide that by the billing cycle months in every column and return the value in cell D11 to P11.

If the formula returns a number greater than zero, then the billing is not required. If the formula returns a zero, then it's time to bill.

In cells D16 to P16, a simple message can be created to flag when to bill.

PRODUCT()

The PRODUCT() function is used to multiply data together. This function is an alternative to writing a lengthy formula summing several numbers.

The syntax for the PRODUCT() function is as follows:

=PRODUCT(Number1,Number2,...Number255)

In Figure 3-27, I have shown how you can simply set up a table and multiply the numbers consecutively.

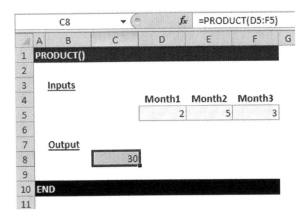

Figure 3-27. This figure shows the PRODUCT() function in use

Figure 3-28 shows the alternative to using the PRODUCT() function.

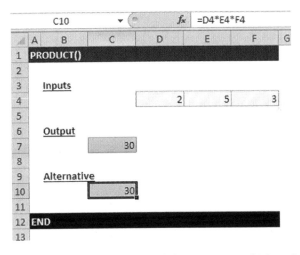

Figure 3-28. The alternative to the PRODUCT() function is to multiply each number individually

You can probably see already that the formula in Figure 3-27 can be clumsy. If you have a large set of numbers, it will very quickly become a lengthy and quite ugly formula.

SUM()

The SUM() function provides a quick way to total columns or rows of numbers in an Excel worksheet, thus creating a total as in Figure 3-29. For modeling purposes, this is a must function—there is no possible way that any model can be without a number of SUM() functions. It is the most widely used Excel function. If you have not yet come across it, then this is where you need to make sure you understand how to use it.

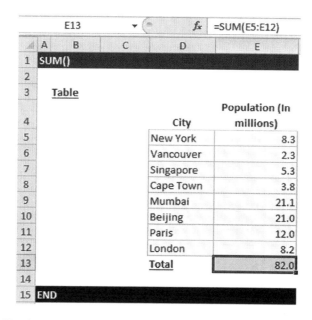

Figure 3-29. This figure shows the SUM() function in use

The syntax for the SUM() function is as follows:

$$=SUM(Number1, Number2, ... Number255)$$

The SUM() function is very versatile and quite simple. It's just a matter of highlighting all the cells or numbers that you want to total.

Logical Functions

These functions return only a true or false variety. They can be used individually or combined with one or more other functions, such as the IF function.

Note Excel has seven built-in logical functions; these are AND(), FALSE(), IF(), IFERROR(), NOT(), OR(), and TRUE(). These functions appear on the drop-down menu with the Logical command button. The Logical command button is found on the Formula tab of the ribbon. All the logical functions return either the logical TRUE or logical FALSE when their functions are evaluated.

AND()

To determine whether the output will be TRUE or FALSE, the AND() function evaluates at least one other mathematical expression located in another cell in the spreadsheet. The AND() function on its own is not very useful and is generally used in combination with the IF statement.

Generally, the syntax you would use is as follows:

$$=AND(logical\text{-}statement.)$$

- *Logical* refers to the cell reference that is being checked. Up to 255 logical values can be entered into the function.

- *Statement* is an expression of a condition that should be met by the logical.

In the example in Figure 3-30, the AND() function is combined with the IF() function for evaluating the final answer. Notice the formula construction and the use of the brackets.

| G10 | f_x | =IF(AND(F10>C5,F10<=D5),E5,IF(AND(F10>=C6,F10<=D6),E6,0)) |

	A	B	C	D	E	F	G	H	I
1	AND()								
2									
3		Grade Table							
4			Salary from	Salary To	Grade				
5			0	25,000	1				
6			25,001	50,000	2				
7									
8		Table							
9			Name	Gender	Age	Salary	Grade		
10			Mindy	F	25	23,400	1		
11			John	M	28	26,210	2		
12			Pat	F	31	32,900	2		
13			Anthony	M	24	21,300	1		
14			Cindy	F	31	35,400	2		
15			Tom	M	23	22,740	1		
16			Richard	M	24	22,108	1		
17			Claire	F	29	34,500	2		
18			Sanjeev	M	32	32,750	2		
19									
20	END								
21									

Figure 3-30. Using the AND() function with the IF() function is shown here

The formula in Figure 3-30 is already starting to look complex, and it's best to avoid embedding any more levels of IFs and ANDs. The objective is to find at which grade employees should be placed based on their salary. This is a classic IF() and AND() situation. Let's take a closer look at the formula:

=IF(AND(F10>C5,F10<=D5),E5,IF(AND(F10>=C6,F10<=D6),E6,0))

If the value in cell C5 is less than the value in cell F10

And

If the value in cell D5 is greater than or equal to the value in cell F10

Then

The solution can be found cell E5.

=IF(AND(F10>C5,F10<=D5),E5,IF(AND(F10>=C6,F10<=D6),E6,0))

Or else

If the value in cell C6 is less than or equal to the value in cell F10

And

If the value in cell D6 is greater than or equal to the value in cell F10

Then

The solution can be found in cell E6.

=IF(AND(F10>C5,F10<=D5),E5,**IF(AND(F10>=C6,F10<=D6),E6,**0))

Otherwise, the solution is zero.

=IF(AND(F10>C5,F10<=D5),E5,IF(AND(F10>=C6,F10<=D6),E6,**0**))

The formula will look through all the permutations, select the one that matches exactly with the two statements, and then find the solution cell. If none of the statements match, then it will make the solution zero.

I have mentioned about making sure the IF statements do not become too embedded and hence too long, but I will mention it again because it's such an important principle. Do not be tempted to make long IF statements even if you can. It's not a sign of cleverness—it's a sign of weakness for a modeler. Take a look at the formula in Figure 3-31. Imagine that you have hundreds of these to audit and correct. How much fun would that be?

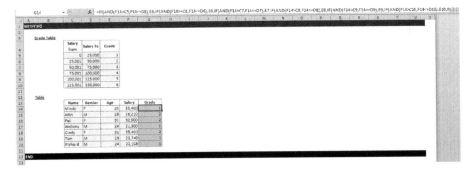

Figure 3-31. This is an example of an embedded IF() statement with the AND() function. It's so complex that it's unreadable

OR()

The OR() function is similar in every way to the AND() function except for the logic of what it is looking at. While the AND() function checks that two points (cells) both satisfy the criteria, the OR() function will check two points but is satisfied if just one of the points matches the criteria.

The syntax for the OR() function is as follows:

$$=OR(logical\text{-}1, logical\text{-}2, \ldots logical\text{-}255)$$

Figure 3-32 is exactly like the AND() function from Figure 3-30, with just the change of the AND() to an OR(). While the AND() is looking to fulfill two conditions, the OR() looks for just one condition to be fulfilled.

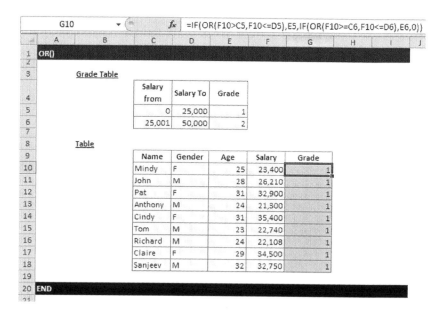

Figure 3-32. The IF() function is used with the OR() function to find the grade but not so successfully

ISERROR()

Prior to wrapping up logical functions, there is one other function that really should be part of the modeler's armory and that is the ISERROR() function. In essence, this function checks a cell or range to see if there is some sort of error. In other words, the values that are expected to be in that location are somehow not coming through as they should.

The syntax you would use is as follows:

$$=ISERROR(value)$$

The most effective way to use this function is with the IF statement. This way, you can check to see if there is an error in a specific cell and then return a specific message if an error is found. A different message could be returned if there is no error. In the following example, Excel will check to see if there is an error in cell G6. If there is, it will return the text "Problem." If not, it will return "OK".

$$=IF(ISERROR(G6, "Problem", "OK")$$

Functions That Use Arrays

There are some functions in excel that are designed to work with a list of data, called an array. These functions have the advantage in that one formula can read a whole list of data and perform a calculation on the whole list if required.

SUMPRODUCT()

The SUMPRODUCT() function is one of the most powerful summing formulas in Excel, but it does require some getting used to in order to use it effectively. At the outset, the SUMPRODUCT() formula may not seem like all that useful. However, once you understand how Excel works with lists (or arrays) of data, the relevance of this function becomes clear.

■ **Note** In Excel, the term "array" signifies a range, a list, or even a group of related data values. The crucial word is "related".

The syntax is as follows:

$$=SUMPRODUCT\ (list\ 1, list\ 2, \dots)$$

				fx	=SUMPRODUCT(F5:F13,G5:G13)
G16					

	A	B	C	D	E	F	G
1	SUMPRODUCT()						
2							
3		Table					
4				Name	Gender	Age	Days Worked	Daily Rate
5				Mindy	F	25	19.0	250
6				John	M	28	19.0	270
7				Pat	F	31	19.0	290
8				Anthony	M	24	16.5	195
9				Cindy	F	31	18.0	250
10				Tom	M	23	19.0	200
11				Richard	M	24	17.5	180
12				Claire	F	29	17.5	210
13				Sanjeev	M	32	17.5	250
14								
15								
16			What is the total cost for the month?					38,108
17								
18	END							

Figure 3-33. This figure shows the use of the SUMPRODUCT() function

Let's take a closer look at the formula:

=SUMPRODUCT(F5:F13,G5:G13)

Take the range (array) starting from cell F5 and ending at cell F13.

=SUMPRODUCT(F5:F13,G5:G13**)**

Then take the range starting from cell G5 and ending at cell G13.

=SUMPRODUCT(F5:F13,**G5:G13**)

And

Match the corresponding cells in the two ranges and multiply each of the days worked by its corresponding rate. Then produce the total for all the cells.

=SUMPRODUCT(F5:F13,G5:G13).

The alternative is to multiply out each row's days worked × daily rate individually and then add the results together using a SUM() function as in Figure 3-34.

H5					f_x	=F5*G5		
	A	B	C	D	E	F	G	H
1	SUMPRODUCT()							
2								
3		Table						
4			Name	Gender	Age	Days worked	Daily Rate	Total
5			Mindy	F	25	19.0	250	4,750
6			John	M	28	19.0	270	5,130
7			Pat	F	31	19.0	290	5,510
8			Anthony	M	24	16.5	195	3,218
9			Cindy	F	31	18.0	250	4,500
10			Tom	M	23	19.0	200	3,800
11			Richard	M	24	17.5	180	3,150
12			Claire	F	29	17.5	210	3,675
13			Sanjeev	M	32	17.5	250	4,375
14								38,108
15								
16		What is the total cost for the month?					38,108	
17								
18								

Figure 3-34. An alternative to the SUMPRODUCT would to multiply the days worked x daily rate for each row and then get the total 38,108

From the examples in Figures 3-32 and 3-33, it should be clear that although it's possible to achieve the same results using other means, the SUMPRODUCT() is a powerful and efficient function and requires fewer computing resources. In this example, I would be using ten SUM() functions to get the same results as one SUMPRODUCT() function.

The SUMPRODUCT() is reliant on matching arrays or matching lists, just make sure that the arrays are the same sizes. For instance, in Figure 3-34, they start at row 5 and end at row 13. If any of these is a different size, you will receive a result but it will be incorrect. This is called a "pointing error." Pointing errors are incredibly easy to make, particularly if you are in a rush. The best way to avoid such a mistake is to make sure you visibly mark out the array so that you can see it on your screen and avoid manually typing the row number and column letter.

Working with Custom Functions or UDFs

In this section, I will take you through using user-defined functions (UDFs). These are functions that the modeler creates using the VBA editor within Excel and can then use in the model alongside the built-in functions.

What Are UDFs?

Excel typically has over 300 built-in functions, some of which we have already covered in this chapter. But as you build up your experience of financial modeling and also with using Excel, you will come across situations where these built-in functions will not provide a satisfactory solution to a modeling problem. As a modeler, it is beneficial at this point if you are able to turn your hand to creating custom functions, known as user-defined functions (UDFs).

UDFs can be used the same way you would use the SUM() function or some other built-in Excel function. They are not complex; however, to create them you must have some level of VBA coding experience. Even if you are familiar with the Excel macro recorder, you will find that the recorder is not suitable for recording UDFs. Therefore, you have to create the UDF yourself. (If you are unfamiliar with VBA, Chapter 12 contains a primer that can get you started.) Nevertheless, this is not to say that you cannot copy and paste bits of a recorded macro into your UDF. UDFs do not have the same flexibility as a standard procedure (VBA) and have many limitations including the following:

- A UDF cannot alter the structure of a worksheet, such as changing the worksheet name, turning off gridlines, protecting the worksheet, and so forth.

- A UDF cannot change a physical characteristic of a cell, including the one that houses the UDF. You cannot use a UDF to change the font color, background color, and so forth of any cell.

- A UDF cannot be used to try and change any part of another cell in any way. This means a UDF cannot place a value into any other cell except the cell housing the UDF.

- A UDF cannot use many of Excel's built-in features, such as auto filters, advanced filters, find, and replace. You can use a UDF to call (run) another standard procedure, but if you do the standard procedure will then be under the same restrictions as the UDF itself.

- When a UDF has a run-time error (that is, it cannot be executed), there are no messages produced. This means you will not know that something has gone wrong, except that there will be an error in your model such as #VALUE. You need to be aware of this issue and either develop a mechanism that will react to any errors or have some documentation in the model that instructs users what they should do if an error occurs.

- UDFs are less efficient than the 300 or so built-in Excel functions because the built-in functions are written using C++, which is a faster language than visual basic.

All this negativity may leave you thinking, "What is the use of UDFs then?" But let me assure you that they can and do come in very handy, as long as you are aware of the restrictions imposed upon them.

When used in the correct context, you can build your own library of functions that are on hand to accompany your models that just aren't available to other users of Excel. The next part of the chapter will include examples of UDFs that I have used previously and continue to use in model building.

Tip Your UDF can be found using the paste function wizard (Shift+F3). Select "User Defined" which is near the bottom of the left-hand window and your UDF will appear on the right-hand window.

When Would You Design and Use UDFs?

When modeling, there will come a time when a UDF is really the only way to get past a particular issue. UDFs will need to be designed and created in the following situations:

- When you need a complex or custom math function that is not available, for instance, a tax calculation based on regional locations.

- When you need to simplify formulas that would otherwise be extremely long "mega formulas", such as to get around using a nested IF statement.

- When you need to use diagnostics such as checking cell formats.

- When you need to use custom text manipulation.

- When you need to include advanced array formulas and matrix functions.

Caution Be careful about using custom functions in spreadsheets that you need to share with others. If the recipients do not have your add-in, the functions will not work when they use the spreadsheet. In such a situation, you will need to send additional details to the recipients to install the add-in.

LINKADDRESS()

The LinkAddress() function is used to show the address details to a cell that has been hyperlinked. In other words, it will show which location the hyperlink is pointing to. Often a model will have hyperlinks to various source references and to other files and documents as a way of providing background information about the model to the user. The fact that Excel has no native function to replicate this link address means that this function is very practical when you need to alert the model user that certain cells include a hyperlink and the details. Another reason is that the place where the hyperlink was originally pointing to may have been deleted or has moved, in which case the hyperlink will not work. However, by giving the details to the user, the user can use that information to follow up. This function is also very useful for auditing. For example, I use this as a tool to check the status of all the hyperlinks when I perform model audits as in Figure 3-35.

	A	B	C	D	E	F	G	H
	H5		fx	=LinkAddress(B5,"")				
1	UDF							
2								
3								
4		Reference	Contact	Assumption	Owner	Date		Ref Trace
5		Sc&St.doc v1.1	DT	Contract will run for 4 years	J.Perkins	Jul-21-2013		Archive\financial_modeling_Repository.docx
6								
7								
8								
9	END							

Figure 3-35. A custom function is included to give details of where the hyperlink is pointing

The syntax for this function is as follows:

$$=Linkaddress(Cell, [Default\ Value])$$

- *Cell* is the cell that contains the hyperlink.

- *Default value* is the value that you want returned if the function finds no hyperlink. This can be anything of your choice. But keep in mind if it is not a numerical value, then place it in quotation marks (" ").

The quickest and most efficient method of learning how to create UDFs is to look at the code to an actual working function. In this section, I have included the actual code for the UDFs, which you should examine and try out, and get an understanding of how they work. In time, you could expand the code or even make it more efficient.

The Code

```
Function LinkAddress(cell As range, _
                     Optional default_value As Variant)
    'Lists the Hyperlink Address for a Given Cell
    'If cell does not contain a hyperlink, return default_value
    If (cell.range("A1").Hyperlinks.Count <> 1) Then
        LinkAddress = default_value
    Else
        LinkAddress = cell.range("A1").Hyperlinks(1).Address
    End If
End Function
```

You can use the code directly from this book and paste it into your VBA editor. In your Excel model, press ALT+F11 to open the VBA editor, in the menu choose Insert then menu, then add a module and paste this code directly into the windowpane.

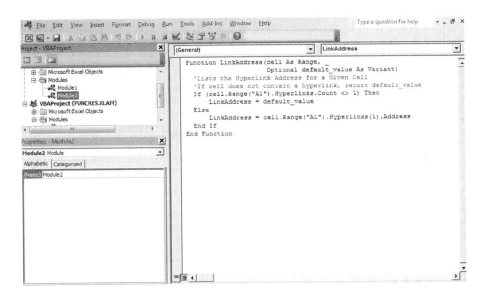

Figure 3-36. The VBA editor is where the UDFs are created by inserting a module and typing code into the editing screen

EFFINDEX()

I have used the EFFINDEX() function to demonstrate how a simple function can be created and can make such a difference. This function takes two values, the demand and the supply, which can both be any value. The demand will then be divided by the supply to give an index. The real power from the EFFINDEX() function is how it treats the values should one of them be a zero. In Excel, when you create a formula that uses divisors, you need to consider what will happen if the divisor has met a zero. Excel will always give an error in this circumstance, placing the #VALUE error where your result should have been. The problem will become exacerbated if that cell with the error has any other cells that are dependent on its value. If so, your model will quickly become strewn with error.

The way to avoid such a situation is to create a formula with an IF() statement and an Error function together. Take a look at Figures 3-37a and 3-37b.

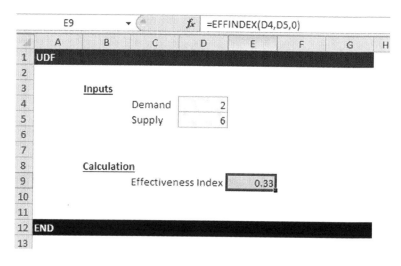

Figure 3-37a. The EFFINDEX() function with a standard divisor is shown here

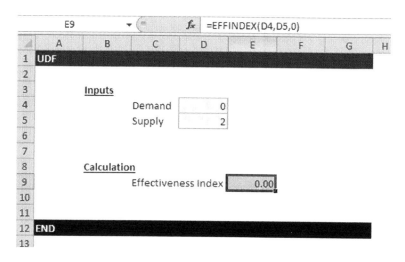

Figure 3-37b. The EFFINDEX() function with a zero divisor, but it shows the default_value and not an error

The syntax for the custom UDF is as follows:

=EFFINDEX(demand,supply,[default_value])

- *Demand* is any value that gives the total demand.
- *Supply* is any value that gives the total supply.
- *Default_value* chooses the default should the answer be an error.

In Figure 3-37a, the demand is simply divided by the supply to give an index of 0.33 or 33%. Notice the default_value is a zero. In Figure 3-37b, we can see how that default_value comes into play, because ordinarily the effectiveness index would have shown a #VALUE error.

I have included the code you will need to create the EFFINDEX() custom function.

The Code

```
Function EFFINDEX(demand As Variant, supply As Variant, _
          Optional default_value As Variant) As Variant
'Effectiveness Index (EFFINDEX)
    If IsMissing(default_value) Then
        default_value = "n/a"
    End If
    If IsNumeric(demand) And IsNumeric(supply) Then
        If supply = 0 Then
            EFFINDEX = demand
            Exit Function
        Else
            EFFINDEX = demand / supply
            Exit Function
        End If
    End If
    EFFINDEX = default_value
End Function
```

SUMCOLOR()

This SUMCOLOR() function can sum data based on the color. Although I have included this function to demonstrate custom functions, I would not recommend using it in models as standard sum for colors. Why? It is vulnerable to some serious problems based on changes to the Excel color palette. However, this function is very useful for auditing financial models. It allows the auditor to color-code specific data and then make checks on that data. Therefore, this is also an example of a function that should be used outside of the model but remains useful to the modeler.

Caution The colors that you will see in your Excel environment are not necessarily the same for all Excel users. This is called the color palette, which can be changed by users and sometimes will change itself depending on your desktop profile. If you sum by colors, just be aware that you are reliant on their colors being exactly the same on their computer as they were on yours.

The syntax for this function is as follows:

$$=SumColor(ColorRange, SumRange)$$

- *ColorRange* is the list or range of cells that has been colored.

- *SumRange* is the list or range of cells you need to get the sum value.

The example in Figure 3-38 demonstrates how the formula works. This function is also useful because you can tailor it to your specifics for modeling. It doesn't need to be about colors. Once you gain experience creating these functions, you can use such a function to sum on any manner of criteria like names, locations, formula types, dates, and so forth. It can even be changed to do a count rather than a sum.

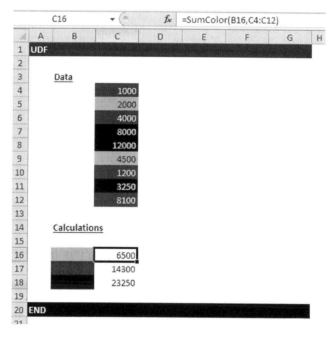

Figure 3-38. The SUMCOLOR() function in use is shown here

The Code
```
Function SumColor(rColor As Range, rSumRange As Range)
'Sums cells based on a specified fill Color.
Dim rCell As Range
Dim iCol As Integer
Dim vResultiCol = rColor.Interior.ColorIndex
For Each rCell In rSumRange
If rCell.Interior.ColorIndex = iCol Then
vResult = WorksheetFunction.Sum(rCell) + vResult
End If
Next rCell
        SumColor = vResult
End Function
```

▓ **Caution**   As this function stands, it won't be much use for summing text; you will need to make some considerable adaptations should you wish to go that route. Summing on text is something I would not choose to do as it's a sure way of rubbishing a model. However, that is my opinion and I do know some modelers who have used text summing successfully. Good luck!

SUMTB()

I have included the SUMTB() function (SumTopBottom) because it's so useful for financial dashboards. For some reason, users of financial models really like to see results that show the top performing and the bottom performing results, that is, the top 5 or bottom 10. Trying to produce this using Excel's advanced filters is awkward. The SUMTB() function also has a more complex deeper VBA coding, which I will explain more in chapter 12.

The syntax is as follows:

=SumTB($A$2:$A$100,10) For top 10

=SumTB($A$2:$A$100,10,TRUE) For bottom 10

I have included the code for the SUMTB()

The Code
```
Function SUMTB(rRange As Range, N As Long, Optional bBottomN As Boolean) As
Single
Dim strAddress As String
On Error Resume Next
strAddress = rRange.Address
```

```
    If bBottomN = False Then
        SUMTB = Evaluate("=SUMPRODUCT((" _
& strAddress & ">=LARGE(" & strAddress & "," & X & "))*(" & strAddress &
"))")
    Else
       SUMTB = Evaluate("=SUMPRODUCT((" _
& strAddress & "<=SMALL(" & strAddress & "," & X & "))*(" & strAddress &
"))")
    End If
End Function
```

ISDATE()

One real gap in Excel is that it has nothing to check the date cell format. You will find that it is very useful in models to have some method of checking if an input cell that is expecting a date has actually received a date from the user. Dates are a cause of errors in models due to problems with syntax and also typing mistakes. I use the ISDATE() function as an error check to give the users a warning if there is a problem with the date that they have input-ted. The ISDATE() function is also used to check if a cell contains a date, as in Figure 3-39a, and if not then the function will return a FALSE. Figure 3-39b shows that it will return TRUE if it has a date.

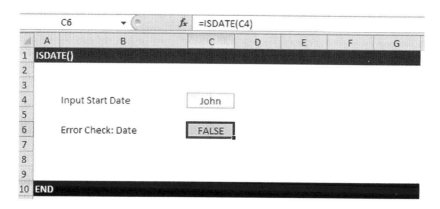

Figure 3-39a. The ISDATE() function has verified that cell C4 is not a date

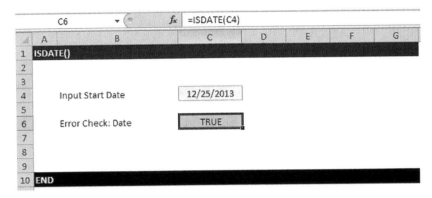

Figure 3-39b. The ISDATE() function has verified that cell C4 is a date

The syntax for the ISDATE() function is as follows:

$$=ISDATE(Cell)$$

The Code
```
Function ISDATE(cell) As Boolean
ISDATE = VBA.ISDATE(cell)
End Function
```

▓ **Caution** Changing the format between text and number (or between number and text) will have no effect on data already entered. If the cell was already formatted as a number and that format was in effect, then you can change to another number format and it will be immediately effective.

WORKSHEETSTATS()

This formula is very useful for producing stats on the data in a worksheet. I use this as part of the documentation in each worksheet as it keeps a record of any changes and the contents of the worksheet and gives valuable feedback to the model user. The results can be seen in Figure 3-40. This is a relatively long function, and my main purpose for including it is to provide some achievement goal. Keep in mind that if you use this function on a blank worksheet, the results will not be accurate. Only use it when there is actual data in the worksheet.

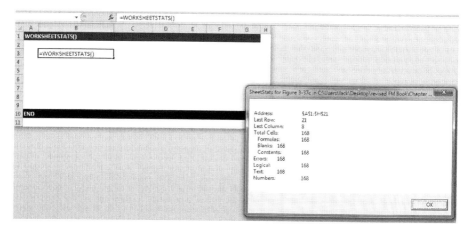

Figure 3-40. The WORKSHEETSTATS() function includes a pop-up message box with information on the worksheet

The syntax for the WORKSHEETSTATS() function is as follows:

=WORKSHEETSTATS()

The Code

```
Function WORKSHEETSTATS()
Set rng1 = ActiveSheet.UsedRange
On Error Resume Next
numConstants = rng1.SpecialCells(xlCellTypeConstants).Count
If Err <> 0 Then numConstants = 0: Err = 0
numerrors = rng1.SpecialCells(xlCellTypeConstants, xlErrors).Count
If Err <> 0 Then numerrors = 0: Err = 0
numLogical = rng1.SpecialCells(xlCellTypeConstants, xlLogical).Count
If Err <> 0 Then numLogical = 0: Err = 0
numText = rng1.SpecialCells(xlCellTypeConstants, xlTextValues).Count
If Err <> 0 Then numText = 0: Err = 0
numNumbers = rng1.SpecialCells(xlCellTypeConstants, xlNumbers).Count
If Err <> 0 Then numNumbers = 0: Err = 0
numformulas = rng1.SpecialCells(xlCellTypeFormulas).Count
If Err <> 0 Then numformulas = 0: Err = 0
numBlanks = rng1.SpecialCells(xlBlanks).Count
If Err <> 0 Then numBlanks = 0: Err = 0

Msg = "Address:      " & Chr(9) & rng1.Address & Chr(10) & _
      "Last Row:     " & Chr(9) & rng1.Rows(rng1.Rows.Count).Row & Chr(10) & _
```

```
        "Last Column: " & Chr(9) & rng1.Columns(rng1.Columns.Count).Column &
Chr(10) & _
        "Total Cells: " & Chr(9) & rng1.Count & Chr(10) & _
        "   Formulas: " & Chr(9) & numformulas & Chr(10) & _
        "   Blanks:   " & Chr(9) & numBlanks & Chr(10) & _
        "   Constants:" & Chr(9) & numConstants & Chr(10)

Mg2 = "Errors:     " & Chr(9) & numerrors & Chr(10) & _
      "Logical:    " & Chr(9) & numLogical & Chr(10) & _
      "Text:       " & Chr(9) & numText & Chr(10) & _
      "Numbers:    " & Chr(9) & numNumbers

    title1 = "SheetStats for " & Application.ActiveSheet.Name & _
    " in " & Application.ActiveWorkbook.FullName

    iANS = MsgBox(Msg & Mg2, , title1)

End Function
```

Typical Modeling Issues and How to Address Them with Functions

There are any number of issues that arise with modeling. In fact, a large part of how to model is based on dealing with potential issues, predicting their likelihood and severity, and modeling for these occurrences. In this chapter, we have looked at functions, which in general will cover the vast majority of issues that will arise. There is one that I will cover now, specifically because it is perhaps the single most destructive problem that can occur, and unfortunately it is very common.

Dealing with Text When You Need Values

One of the most common issues in any model is predicting how the user will respond to the inputs. Will they follow the protocol or deviate? For instance, if a user input cell requires a number (value) and the user places text, how should we deal with this as the model calculation will have corrupted data? Are there any functions we can use to mitigate? To explore this issue more and learn how to mitigate, I have included a series of examples from Figures 3-41 to 3-46.

Figure 3-41 is a small model, and the objective is to derive the price. I am asking the user to input the revenue and profit margin for each of the months. The price is a simple calculation: revenue × margin. Notice that I have used a color style, just as we discussed in Chapter 2 about best practice.

	L1			f_x							
	A	B	C	D	E	F	G	H	I	J	K
1	Layout										
2											
3		Inputs									
4			Month	Jan-13	Feb-13	Mar-13	Apr-13	May-13	Jun-13	Jul-13	
5			Revenue (Value)	34,000	39,500	38,200	38,350	38,120	39,400	40,020	
6			Profit Margin in %	7.0%	7.0%	7.0%	7.0%	7.0%	7.0%	7.0%	
7											
8											
9		Calculation									
10			Month	Jan-13	Feb-13	Mar-13	Apr-13	May-13	Jun-13	Jul-13	
11			Revenue	34,000	39,500	38,200	38,350	38,120	39,400	40,020	
12			Profit Margin	7.0%	7.0%	7.0%	7.0%	7.0%	7.0%	7.0%	
13			Price	36,380	42,265	40,874	41,035	40,788	42,158	42,821	
14											
15		Output									
16				Jan-13	Feb-13	Mar-13	Apr-13	May-13	Jun-13	Jul-13	
17			Price	36,380	42,265	40,874	41,035	40,788	42,158	42,821	
18			Cumulative Price	36,380	78,645	119,519	160,554	201,342	243,500	286,321	
19											
20	END										
21											

Figure 3-41. The inputs, calculations, and outputs are shown in this figure

In Figure 3-41, the profit margin expects a value that should be a percentage. Instead of a number, the user has used a text and has actually written "7 percent." The effect of this text entry can be seen in the calculations in rows 11 and 12 with an error now creeping into the model. When we reach the outputs, the error is now firmly entrenched into the model. This is not acceptable modeling, but unfortunately this is a very common occurrence. If the user is not fully versed with all the inputs in the model, this issue will occur. Fortunately for this situation, there are some options we can take to minimize the effect this issue can have on the model.

	A	B	C	D	E	F	G	H	I	J
1	**Layout**									
2										
3		**Inputs**								
4			Month	Jan-13	Feb-13	Mar-13	Apr-13	May-13	Jun-13	Jul-13
5			Revenue (Value)	34,000	39,500	38,200	38,350	38,120	39,400	40,020
6			Profit Margin in %	7 per cent	7 per cent	7 per cent	7 per cent	7 per cent	7 per cent	7 per cent
7										
8										
9		**Calculation**								
10			Month	Jan-13	Feb-13	Mar-13	Apr-13	May-13	Jun-13	Jul-13
11			Revenue	34,000	39,500	38,200	38,350	38,120	39,400	40,020
12			Profit Margin	7 per cent	7 per cent	7 per cent	7 per cent	7 per cent	7 per cent	7 per cent
13			Price	#VALUE!	#VALUE!	#VALUE!	#VALUE!	#VALUE!	#VALUE!	#VALUE!
14										
15		**Output**								
16				Jan-13	Feb-13	Mar-13	Apr-13	May-13	Jun-13	Jul-13
17			Price	#VALUE!	#VALUE!	#VALUE!	#VALUE!	#VALUE!	#VALUE!	#VALUE!
18			Cumulative Price	#VALUE!	#VALUE!	#VALUE!	#VALUE!	#VALUE!	#VALUE!	#VALUE!
19										
20	**END**									

Figure 3-42. The inputs have text entered in value cells

In Figure 3-43, in order to help the user input the correct type of data, I have created a data validation, which can be found in the data menu. With the data validation, you can stipulate the data type that can be entered in each cell and only that data type will be allowed. In this case, I have created a validation for a decimal between 0 and 1, which will be a percentage (0% to 100%).

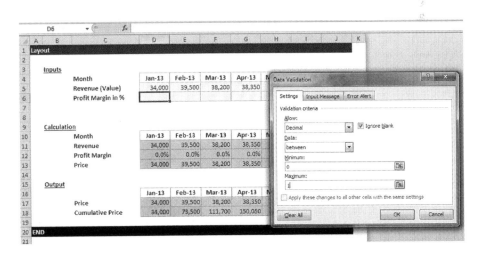

Figure 3-43. Data validation has been introduced into the model in this figure

The next step after creating a data validation is to have some visual error check to alert the model user that there is an issue with the data, as in Figure 3-44. In this case, I have created an IF statement with the ISNUMBER() function. This function checks that the cells in row 5 are numbers. If so, the formula returns a 0; if not, it returns a 1. By using this type of error check, I can provide a visual guide to the user that something in the inputs is incorrect. Now that I have two solutions to the issue—the data validation (Figure 3-43) and the error check (Figure 3-44)—it would be reasonable to assume I have done what I can to mitigate the value/text problem.

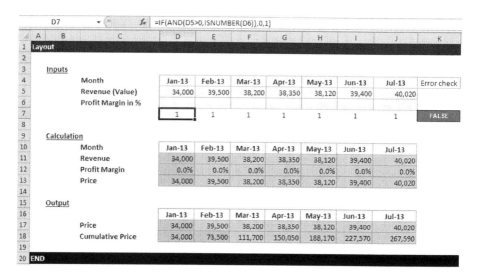

Figure 3-44. Error checks have been added into the model in this figure

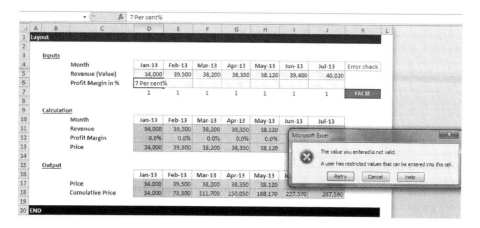

Figure 3-45. The error check and data validation are used in combination to give maximum feedback

The combination of the data validation and the error check will result in a message pop-up as in Figure 3-44, which will need some feedback from the user in order to continue with using the model.

To continue with no issues, users would need to make sure all possible errors are eradicated, whereby they would receive a TRUE check with no validation pop-up messages as in Figure 3-46.

M1		f_x								
	C	D	E	F	G	H	I	J	K	L
1										
2										
3										
4	Month	Jan-13	Feb-13	Mar-13	Apr-13	May-13	Jun-13	Jul-13	Error check	
5	Revenue (Value)	34,000	39,500	38,200	38,350	38,120	39,400	40,020		
6	Profit Margin in %	5.0%	5.0%	5.0%	5.0%	5.0%	5.0%	5.0%		
7		0	0	0	0	0	0	0	TRUE	
8										
9	n									
10	Month	Jan-13	Feb-13	Mar-13	Apr-13	May-13	Jun-13	Jul-13		
11	Revenue	34,000	39,500	38,200	38,350	38,120	39,400	40,020		
12	Profit Margin	5.0%	5.0%	5.0%	5.0%	5.0%	5.0%	5.0%		
13	Price	35,700	41,475	40,110	40,268	40,026	41,370	42,021		
14										
15										
16		Jan-13	Feb-13	Mar-13	Apr-13	May-13	Jun-13	Jul-13		
17	Price	35,700	41,475	40,110	40,268	40,026	41,370	42,021		
18	Cumulative Price	35,700	77,175	117,285	157,553	197,579	238,949	280,970		
19										
20										

Figure 3-46. The inputs now have error checking and validations

This example was illustrative, but I should add that most issues in financial models can be solved in this manner with the use of some functions and error checking.

Case Study: Using Modeling Functions and Tools

This last part of the chapter is a case study to examine a specific situation that is very likely to occur in financial models and particularly in valuation models.

Here is the brief:

Create a model template that will demonstrate how the capital budgeting can be performed in a model.

Let's begin by going over some of the terminology that will be used:

- Capital flow is the amount of set-up money injected into a project.

- Cash flow frequency is the time periods that money inflowing is measured.

- Discount rate is the rate of interest that investors demand from the project.

- Monthly income is the cash flows that occur from a project (not profit).

- Net Present Value (NPV) compares the value of money today to the value of that same money in the future.

Don't worry if you don't understand the financial aspects at this stage. An introduction to finance and accounting for modelers is included in Chapter 8. For this case study, just concentrate on the formula usage and the layout. Figures 3-47 and 3-48 will be used as examples.

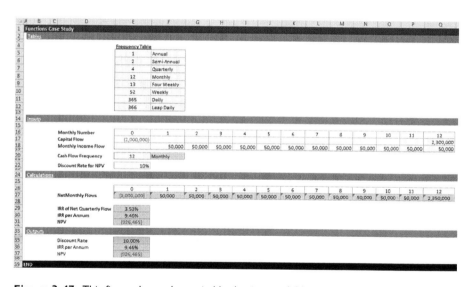

Figure 3-47. This figure shows the capital budgeting model layout

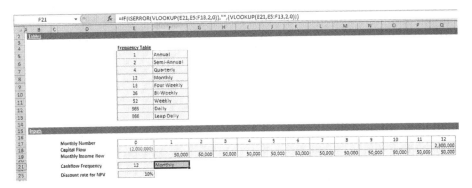

Figure 3-48. The VLOOKUP() function is encased within an IF() statement together with an ISERROR() function in order to catch errors in cell E21

The layout has been sectioned into inputs (user inputs), calculations (workings), and outputs. Inputs are presented in the yellow cells, and calculations are in the gray cells. Notice that cell E21 has yellow shading and a green border; this is a drop-down menu and is signified as such by the green border. Looking at Figure 3-48, you will note that a VLOOKUP() function has been used, but it has been encapsulated in the ISERROR() function to catch any errors.

- VLOOKUP() is referencing cell E21 to the frequency table. It's possible that the user could enter a frequency in cell E21 that is not recognized in the frequency table, which would result in an error. Therefore, the ISERROR function is used to return a space should that happen.
- The IRR() function has been used to get the internal rate of return. Fortunately Excel has a built-in formula construct so when you need to get the internal rate of return (IRR), the only modeling concern is to make the layout of the cash flows fit the formula construct. There is one feature of the IRR function that does confuse people, and that is the "guess" that is required. In effect, the function is asking you to guess at what rate the IRR will be (before it gives you the result). When using this function, don't become too concerned about this guess as it won't alter the result significantly unless you have somehow constructed the formula incorrectly.

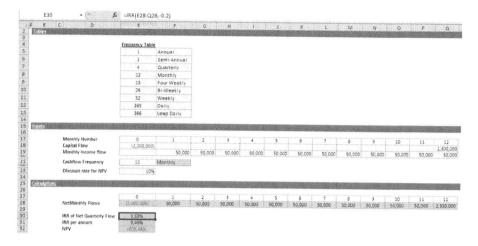

Figure 3-49. The IRR() (internal rate of return) function is shown here in this figure

- The IRR per annum (Figure 3-50) uses the FV math function(the FV() function gives the future value of an investment using the interest that would have accrued) and is derived from the IRR function. This means you will first get the IRR for the frequency and then convert this to per annum using the FV function.

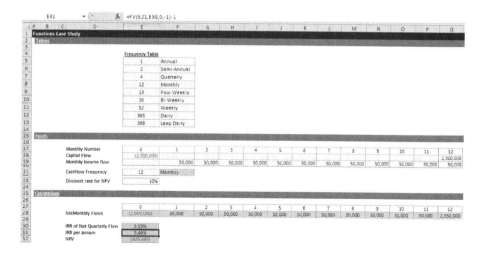

Figure 3-50. The IRR is turned into an annual rate in this model

Generally the IRR() function is used together with the NPV() function, as the NPV (net present value) gives you an indication of how much the investment or project will be worth in the future based on today's money. It is a relatively simple function except for one flaw that you should always be aware of. If you look at Figure 3-51 in the formula construct, you will notice that I have added the capital cash flow to the formula (Year 0, +E28). When using NPV, remember to add back the initial capital, which will always be a negative value even after the discounted cash flow, or you will get a significantly flawed NPV. When making calculations using the NPV() function, you should always remember to add the capital in year 0 to the formula. I have come across numerous models that have omitted this capital addition. Why should this be a problem? Let's just say NPV is used quite widely for financial metrics and comparisons about investments, and the last thing you want to do as a modeler is to give an incorrect result for the NPV. Trust me on that.

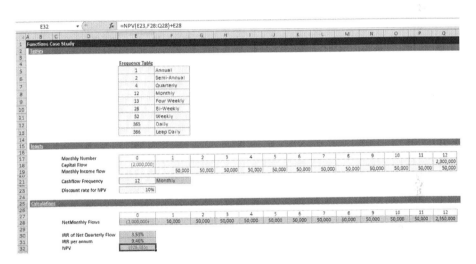

Figure 3-51. This figure illustrates using the NPV() function

This was a long chapter that introduced many technical parts to financial modeling, but it is essential that you meet these functions early. You will hopefully have reached this point having tried some of the functions and are now more familiar with them. Many of these functions will be appearing again and again throughout the book, which is why it's important that you have familiarized yourself with them early on.

Planning Your Model

Based on my fieldwork in financial modeling, my opinion is that the majority of models built have little or no planning involved. There are some cases where there really is no need. But as a financial modeler, at some point, you will need to have some coherent plan for your models, particularly when working on a project where the modeling is only one aspect, such as being on a bid or in a transformation program. It is critical to understand not just how to build models but also how to fulfill all the aspects of planning. This way, you will provide a final model that meets and exceeds user expectations. This chapter introduces the modeling life cycle and will take you through the process of how to manage and take ownership of the entire modeling space.

Introduction to the Financial Modeling Life Cycle

What exactly do I mean by financial modeling life cycle? First, let's take a look at the term "life cycle." It was born from biology, and although there are several definitions, it essentially is about the stages of change during the development of an organism from inception to maturity. Biologists aside, the description would be too literal for financial modeling. However, it does have the hallmarks that we need to create a suitable definition. The key aspects are stages of change during the development, inception, and maturity. Therefore, we can define a financial modeling life cycle as the following:

> The key developmental stages of a financial model that will ensue with the beginning of the initial feasibility and ending with a final living and working functional model.

Take notice of the use of the word "key." There can be a number of development stages to any financial model, but not all of them are necessary and therefore not "key" in every single model. Some stages if omitted would result in a modeling process that is flawed and a final model with key weaknesses. In other words, a substandard model would be the final product.

Here is a list of the ten key development stages:

- Feasibility
- Scope
- Specification & Strategy
- Design
- Build
- Test
- Final Version & Protection
- Document
- Handover & Implementation
- Maintain

While no two financial models are exactly alike, the planning from the beginning to the end resulting in a fully operational model should be the same. The brevity and depth with which each stage is approached will be entirely up to the modeler. As I mentioned before, some may feel they can actually go through the feasibility and scoping stages mentally and even believe the specification stage does not require any formal document. What is important is that these stages are considered, assessed for their usefulness, and then acted upon.

If you are very familiar with financial modeling, you may be wondering why a model audit has not been included in the life cycle. The answer is that it could be, but I have chosen not to since the model audit is not an essential or critical part of the modeling. Obviously it is good to have an audit, but all models do not need to be audited, particularly if they undergo a period of testing. Only the most stringent model audit will actually provide assurance beyond the logical model. In other words, an audit will pinpoint where the model's structure has issues and the problems in the logic, but it will not give assurance as to the materiality of the information about the model, unless the sponsor is willing to pay a considerable fee.

For models that will have an external facing element and will be used to provide information that is sensitive and will be acted upon, I would recommend that the model audit be added to provide assurance above and beyond the testing. But in general, the testing will be sufficient. Figure 4-1 shows the stages in the modeling life cycle.

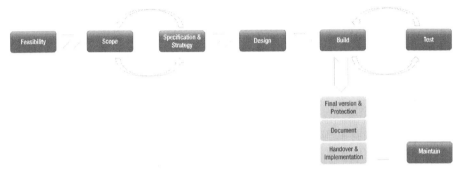

Figure 4-1. This figure is a typical financial modeling life cycle showing the different stages

> ■ **Note** I am aware that there is a large group of organizations who actively use financial models but have no formal review process, which means no one is checking the models. This is not necessarily wrong, as those organizations may not place so much importance on making decisions from models. In that case, any errors would have little magnitude. The concern though is once any of these key development stages are missed, the model process becomes flawed and eventual users of the model will be at the mercy of that planning.

Planning to Build a Model

The planning of the project is actually essential to model building because it helps to eliminate and also mitigate against surprises and issues. There is no worse feeling for a modeler than to find yourself going in circles with no end in sight—either because of problems that have not been resolved, or because the scope of the project has started to creep into something far larger than originally expected with a result that the model becomes large and more complex. The start of planning is marked by a feasibility evaluation of the project, followed by scoping, and then creating the modeling specifications.

To give you just a flavor of the issues modelers are likely to face from the outset of a modeling project, I have described a few in the next few sections. These issues seem to crop up irrespective of where you build the model or what type of model it is, which should be highlighted in the feasibility evaluation.

Is There a Clear Understanding of Cash?

A common mistake in financial models is not having a solid understanding of what cash is and what cash is not. Ask yourself these questions:

- Are revenues cash?
- Are gross margins cash?
- Are profits cash?

The answer to all three of these questions is a resounding "no." If you didn't know this, don't panic. Not everyone in the business world is clear about this either. Then what is cash?

There is no satisfactory answer to the cash question without creating a cash flow statement. Financial models should always makes sure there is a cash flow statement because it's a fundamental requirement of modeling. Without this statement, the user will have difficulty with even performing rudimentary tasks like balancing the balance sheet, estimating availability of funds, or even understanding when the bank account will be in deficit or overdraft. Read through the following example:

Suppose you sell something this month for $100, and the cost of making it was $50 in total. You have to pay your suppliers within 30 days, while the buyer probably won't pay you for at least 60 days. In this case, your revenue for the month was $100, your profit for the month was $50, and your cash flow for the month was zero. Your cash flow for the transaction will be negative $50 next month when you pay your suppliers. Although this example may seem trivial, slight changes to the timing between cash receipt and disbursement, even just a couple of weeks, can bankrupt a business. Therefore, a good model will reflect not only cash flows generated by the organization but also their timing.

How Much Detail Is Required?

When planning, take a look at the financial information that has been requested by the model owner and model users and work out how much detail will be required. For instance, the requirement might be to have a summary level profit and loss (income) statement that just shows revenue, costs of sales and services, expenses, and net profit. Don't be fooled into believing this is really all you will need. My advice is to always plan to build at the detail level; the financials should be constructed from the bottom-up and then validated from the top-down.

A bottom-up model starts with details, such as the types of revenues and when they are invoiced and received, or the different types of expenses and again when to expect to pay them. The top-down validation means that you examine your overall summary and compare it with the bottom-up details to be sure they match.

■ **Note** When I audit a financial model, there are some threads that I look at that will tell me if the model financials have been built with detail or not. One of them is to look at the outputs and see how they have been rounded. Numbers that show neat rounding, for example, staff costs are two million in Year 1 and three million in Year 2, is a sign that the bottom-up approach is missing.

Create Scenario Analysis and Sensitivity Analysis

One of the purposes of good financial models is that they include some scenario and sensitivity analyses showing how your projected results will change if your assumptions turn out to be incorrect. If planned properly, the building of these scenarios and sensitivities will subsequently help the user identify and track the assumptions that can have a material effect on future performance. These can then be validated further during the testing.

■ **Note** Scenario analysis is the process of creating a basic model or base case and then changing all the variables to extremes. One extreme creates the best case while the other develops the worst case, allowing you to see the full range of possible outcomes. If the range between the best and worst case is too large for comfort, more research may be warranted before proceeding.

Performed after a scenario analysis, the sensitivity analysis is similar with one significant difference. Instead of changing all the variables simultaneously, you change one variable at a time to its own best and worst case value and rerun the model. Then reset the assumptions to the base case and go on to the next individual variable, and so on. The result from this series of iterations shows which of the assumptions drives the greatest variation in the results or outputs. These specific variables are the ones the user must control to optimize future results.

Assumptions: How Realistic Are They?

During the planning, it's important to set the tone of how the assumptions for the model are going to be validated. The validation is important from the modeler's perspective, because once that is finalized, the modelers will input the assumptions into the model and will be responsible for how those assumptions are interpreted. The question of ownership of assumptions is critical. While the assumptions will be given to the modelers and therefore will have an owner and contact, once they enter the model the modeler is responsible for having them in there. If you don't understand an assumption that is sitting within your model, it's imperative that you do. Why? Because you will have to validate every assumption in order for the users and owner of the model to have assurance that the model is fit for purpose.

Ironically, validating the assumptions can be time-consuming and requires effort in people management. As a result, it is somewhat common to find good working models where the modeler has not fully validated the assumptions. As a result, the assumptions remain in the model, but there is no rational link with reality. I warn against this practice because it leads to the modeler's integrity being questioned. The assumption validation is a two-way process. First, the modeler collects and organizes the assumptions and then sends them back to the original provider of the information. The provider should then confirm that the information now in the assumptions is valid and can be used in the model. By acquiring this information from the assumption owner, the modeler can subsequently make a more informed opinion on the assumption and start to validate. The validation should be based on getting a second or even a third opinion from different sources. If this is not possible, try to throw the assumptions back to the original owner after some elapsed time to see if the assumptions remain the same.

Modelers need to have a firm grip on the assumptions and be willing to push the owner of the assumptions to move as close to reality as possible. For example, few companies achieve huge growth in revenues, profits, and cash flow after a slower period. Projecting numbers that an organization cannot support is never a good idea. It not only wastes your time but assists people in making ill-informed and hence bad decisions that will have long-term negative perceptions on your modeling ability.

Something to keep in mind is that the majority of people who will be viewing and making decisions based on the outputs will be looking for some input from the modeler as to the profile of the assumptions. For example, they may ask if the assumptions are practical and if so how pragmatic, or are they based on empirical evidence and so forth. While it is valid practice to provide some feedback into the assumptions, stop short of making overall assessments, such as that the assumptions are "aggressive" or "conservative" or even "pessimistic" (even if you truly believe they are.) Why is this restraint needed? By giving a general assessment such as "conservative," you will be creating a message that somehow the assumptions have been massaged to suit the audience, which brings the credibility of the model and the modeler into question.

Furthermore, with these types of assessments, modelers open up themselves to someone in the audience wanting to take a different angle. For example, if you decree that the assumptions are conservative, you may be directed to make them more pessimistic. This does happen and more often than not the modeler is left with trying to shape the results from the model to suit another's views. The solution is to use the scenarios that have been built into the model and create a scenario that shows the pessimistic view without altering the base model assumptions.

▓ **Tip**   The best way to achieve these realistic assumptions is to make sure that you have challenged the assumption owner to give you as much background as possible. Also try and support this feedback with something solid (like past results). In essence, always create a relationship with assumption owners that allows them to help you to substantiate everything they give you.

Missing Key Elements in Financial Statements

Make sure that all the financial statements and outputs conform to *generally accepted accounting principles* (GAAP). For instance, if the organization's financials are caught under *International Financial Reporting Standards* (IFRS) and the model is reporting revenues, then be sure that they conform to the IFRS standards on revenue recognition.

Plan how far the model will project. Will it be three years, five years, or even ten years? Is it possible to project the years? If not, then how credible is the model? With most models, it is common to project out three to five years into the future. And while nobody can see five years into the future, having this projection in the model gives some assurance to the model users and anyone else reading the model that you have thought through the process and validated your initial assumptions.

As much as possible, the financial model should provide benchmark comparisons to past performance or leaders and other competitor analysis. Showing key indicators—liquidity ratio, return on capital employed or revenues per employee, gross margin per employee, gross margin as a percentage of revenues, and various expense ratios—can be very helpful and show that there has been a concerted planning and thought process behind the model build.

Developing a Feasibility Assessment

The modeler should commence a model project with a feasibility assessment of the entire model project. More directly, the modeler must assess the relative merits of building the model with reference to physical constraints, such as resourcing, monetary constraints, and skills availability. This assessment will encapsulate aspects like the following:

- Determine the knowledge and size of the team (it could be just yourself) and the adequacy of the resources.

- Establish the timescales from start to delivery and if they are realistic. You will need to cite examples of other similar projects.

- Evaluate the risks and potential pitfalls of developing such a model.

- Assess the relative importance of the model, such as whether it will be used to make key decisions. Is this a one-time-only model to help in a process? Or is this an ongoing model? You will also need to clarify the key personnel, such as the users, owners, stakeholder(s), sponsors, and those who have a vested interest in providing information for the model.

- Consider the readiness of the project, organization and resources, equipment, and software. In other words, determine how rapidly all of these elements can be mobilized.

- Review the appropriateness of the locations or which will be the ideal location. If there is a lot of in-person communications required, the project will benefit from being close to key personnel.

- Know the cost impact of having or not having the model.

- Determine the skill level of the financial modeler with relation to the project requirements (notice this may need to be performed after the requirements gathering).

- Establish if the deliverables are clearly understood. If not, they will need to be developed and stated manifestly at this stage.

- Consider if this exercise is going to be a team effort. If so, the roles within the team should be very clear at this stage. In addition, the resources and time commitment that will be available during the course of the project should be planned.

Scoping the Modeling Project

The scope is a very critical aspect of the planning. As a modeler, you should insist that you are given a clear and unambiguous communication of the full scope for the model. I reiterate the word "full." This means that not only do you gain understanding of what is in scope, but also crucially what is out of scope. For instance, a scope may state that the model "will be used to support the finance teams to identify the key cost drivers." This statement is short and vague, so it will be your responsibility to tie it down. For instance, in this situation, you could start by addressing these questions:

- Who are the finance teams? They need to be stated either by the team name or the chief contact.

- Are the finance teams responsible for providing the information and data to the model? If not, who will? Does the modeler need to build this information?

- Can we define support? Is this a one-time model for a precise purpose and limited time, or is this an ongoing model that will need to be maintained and refreshed with data?

- Do the cost drivers include resources (staff) time?

Once you have covered just about every conceivable aspect, write a scope document, which will need to be approved by the model sponsor. The document should not be more than two pages and should clearly state what is in scope and what is out of scope. In this document, avoid using vague language. You do not want to open the scope to misinterpretation and cause confusion between the modeler and model sponsor as to what should be delivered.

Note When thinking about what is in scope and what is out of scope, I am reminded of a photographer taking a group photo for a football team. When composing the photo, once the photographer looks through the camera lens, what he sees is in scope. Anything outside of the lens is out of scope. However, the photographer still needs to be aware of what is out of scope because it could affect the photo (for example, a bird moving into view at the last second).

I recommend that as the modeler, even though you may be given the scope, be proactive in the scope document creation. Take responsibility for writing the scope document in order to understand exactly what the full project entails. You will also be able to get some control over scope creep, which is very common during model builds. The scope document is the critical element that you would use to control scope creep with the model sponsor, the stakeholders, and the model users.

▓ **Note**   Scope creep is the continuing growth of the size of a project in an uncontrolled manner and usually occurs when the scope is not accurately defined and communicated. Scope creep should be considered as one of the key risks in the feasibility stage and can have an impact on costs by creating cost overruns. The best place to be as the modeler is to have your scope documented, communicated, and be explicit about the change control, such as creating procedures on how to change the scope.

Keep a copy of the approved document and circulate copies to the sponsor and stakeholders. Also place a summary of the scope in the model where it will be visible, such as a part of the documentation or in the assumptions.

The Specification & Strategy

The specification should be a detailed document with a series of requirements for the model that have been gathered from the eventual model users, model owner, sponsor, and stakeholders.

In this stage, the modeler should identify the output parameters (generally the financial statements) of the model. The modeler should also have a design for the types of calculations that will be used in the model and should assess whether there will be a need for VBA programming. The question of the VBA is important for the reason that not all modelers are competent at coding in VBA. What if VBA coding is required and the modeler does not have the skills to deliver such a model? There answer is to alert the project sponsors about the situation. At the same time, the sponsors should be advised either to bring in a VBA programmer to assist the modeler, or secure a modeler who has the VBA skills. It is also important to identify the inputs required for the financial model. Finally, the model parameter should be identified, and all options should be highlighted.

The specification will be quite detailed and will be the reference template that the modeler will use during the design and build of a financial model. The specification is crucial to the model design and therefore should not be produced to reflect the modeler's point of view. It should instead reflect to a large extent the specification of the stakeholders and the users.

The sponsor of the model who may be a stakeholder should sign off on the specifications before you begin any design and build. This is a critical point because many model designs commence before the specification sign-off, for several reasons such as the sponsor is too busy but wants results immediately. My advice is do not be compromised—this is your design plan and also your checklist when the model is complete. In many ways, this is your insurance against scope creep. If you were a constructor, would you start building some-one's dream house without the architect's plans? Be strong; do it right!

The specification should address the following requirements:

- What is this model for?
- Whom is this model for?
- What should the model do?
- What are the inputs required?
- Where will the data and assumptions come from?
- What business logic is required?
- What level of detail is required for the model?
- What flexibility is required? In other words, what needs to be able to change?
- Who will use it and how? What are their skills?
- How often will it be used, for how long, and how?
- How soon is the model required to be live?

These are the requirements that should be gathered in the early stages of the project. In fact, begin working through these as soon as the scope to the project has been produced. (Always entertain the idea that there is a scope document. This is not the modeler's responsibility to create, but it will be the modeler's responsibility to communicate.) You should be as detailed as possible and remember not to make any of your own assumptions as this impartiality will really help when you design and build.

These requirements should always originate from the people who want the model. The modeler can fill in technical, economic, and resource implications as well as any constraints once base specifications have all been put together.

In the beginning, clearly identify the stakeholders and the sponsor (usually the same person who has asked for the model) and their roles and responsibilities within the project. The sponsor should be able to provide a set of high-level requirements that you can use for the specification, which will be your initial template.

The sponsor's requirements are a key component. Therefore, should the sponsor fail to provide the document, insist that you are given access to someone who can give a clear view of the scope. Under no circumstances should you, the modeler, be pushed to a position of creating an initial specification. If you do, you will then run the risk of a project failure due to unclear specifications and miscommunications from feedback. This aspect will ultimately decide the success of the modeling project.

For all modeling projects (irrespective of size), develop the habit of documenting the specifications and model design because it provides a visible and relatively easy checklist during the testing period. I liken this to a presentation. How can you be sure the presentation has gone to plan without an agenda to refer to?

It is extremely important for the modeler to fully understand the business logic, such as all the business rules that need to go through the model. For instance, many business models involve some type of taxation or accounting for inflation (usually termed "indexation") so that you would expect some rules on how the model will be affected by implementing such rules.

Also be sure to heed the warnings surrounding errors in logic and especially omissions as they are among the hardest to find in any model. Don't underestimate the damage that errors can do to the model and how quickly a modeler's work can be undermined if errors are left unchecked.

In the specification stage, keeping all source documents, files, notes, and discussions is imperative for reference, as these should guide the modeler as to the business logic and model. Keep in mind that ultimately the closing working model will reflect this understanding by the modeler and any weaknesses in the modeler will affect the concluding model. However, it seems obvious that the modeler should maintain a healthy respect for referencing information regularly throughout the project. For example, if you are modeling capital investments, you would need documentation on the actual item's lists, depreciation schedules and valuations, assets conditions, and so forth.

My advice is to keep all documents, review, read, understand, always question, and get confirmations. Never in any circumstance leave yourself in a position where you cannot explain the business or project due to a lack of understanding. If you do, you will eventually be found out. If this occurs very late in the project, the modeler would be expected to take full responsibility for any mistakes in the model that reflect this lack of business understanding. Suffice it to say, every modeler should be covered by professional indemnity insurance.

▨ **Caution**   Any modeler who is involved in undertaking projects on behalf of clients and customers should always have professional indemnity (liability) insurance. This should not be an option but a requirement, and it should be at a level well above $1 million in today's money. Once all the matters of compensation and legal fees are totted up, that is the kind of money that you will need to have.

The Benefits of Model Specification

The discipline of performing a model specification will ensure that you produce a definitive statement of what the model should do and how it will do it. It allows the modeler to take on the most difficult problems associated with the model from the very start of the planning. The specification is the only method that allows model users, the model sponsor, and the modeler to collectively agree what the model will be and how it will be delivered. A successful specification establishes a common understanding of what the model will do.

A model specification will make the testing of the model easier and will also provide an effective means of preaching solutions to any defects detected. It is a clear statement of what the model is doing. The model tester then has to check whether the finished model agrees with the written specification.

Failure to write a model specification will lead to difficulties later in the planning because it won't be clear to the modeler exactly what is required by the model sponsor. The following types of problems can occur:

- More time is needed to build the model because the issues that could have been identified in the specification were not resolved and keep coming back.

- Continual late changes keep occurring in the model logic, not all by the model sponsor or users, but also by the modeler who has failed to come to terms with some of the more difficult issues of the model early enough. This is potentially the greatest single cause of errors in completed models.

- Vague objectives characterize the model. It is easy to start with a small model that aims to solve one problem but ends up with a large model that solves all sorts of other problems, but solves them badly.

Defining Model Outputs

The first stage during the model specification process is to refine the broad output requirements that were defined from the scope stage into defined outputs that the model will produce. Do not underestimate how much time and effort this step can take. On a large project plan, this can be a matter of days and possibly weeks to get a final specification. Note this difference: the scope is about "where do we want to be?" and the defined specifications are about "what do we need to get to where we want to be?"

The simplest method of presenting the model outputs is to produce templates or outline reports using Excel. Outline reports will look like the final output without the data. These outline reports will give everyone involved the best possible idea of what the last outputs will look like early and can also be approved or modified by the model owner. Whenever possible, try to get the model sponsor to produce the outline reports, as this will add to the sign-off of the specification.

This is a stage in which the model sponsor needs to be involved to agree on what information is required in the model reports. Here is a list of typical questions that need to be answered:

- Who is going to use the model reports?

- What purpose is each model report going to serve?

- What is the appropriate level of detail to include on each report?

When you have established an outline for the model reports, you can consider the calculations needed to give you the required outputs.

Defining Calculations: Techniques for the Model Specifications

Developing the calculation rules that define the workings of a model can be difficult, especially when your understanding about the problem to be modeled is vague. That is why the process of defining the model specification will most likely be iterative, as more than one attempt is required before you get it right. In order to develop the calculations, you will need to address the type of information organization you will use. For instance, will the model consist of several tables with data? Will there be user inputs to affect these tables? By thinking through the data, it will become clear about the types of calculations and hence functions and formula that will be required.

For instance, if there will be numerous tables holding data, it is certain that the lookup functions such as MATCH() and INDEX() will be required. Also, if totals are required from these tables, you will not be able to ignore the SUMIF() or COUNTIF() functions.

When defining the calculations, start by listing the functions that will definitely be required. Then list those that will be useful and finally those that will have very minimal usage. In this way, you will have a record later for documenting the calculations used in the model.

Defining the Inputs

Once you have defined the model calculations, the inputs required for the model should be implicit (based on intuition and specification but have not yet been formalized). It is frequently worth considering in more detail what inputs are required and how they are to be sourced. It is never easy defining inputs because by their nature, they rely upon the final user's vision of which sensitivities they will need, which may not be available during the planning. My advice is to look at the outputs, which should have been defined previously. It should be clear from these outputs exactly what types of inputs and sensitivities will be required, although this is also a matter of what level of experience the modeler has of such projects. For instance, if the outputs (reports) have an income statement showing five years of revenues and financials, it is certain that inputs of the selling price for five years will be required.

One method is to list the various inputs and types in a data sheet; you can then map these input items to actual outputs. A data input list of this form is useful for the following reasons:

- Establishes the level of detail required in the input assumptions at an early stage in a form that is easy to communicate.

- Highlights where special effort will be required in data collection and assigns responsibility for producing the data.

- Lists the type of estimate that will be used for each input assumption in the status column. This can help identify the inputs that will be candidates for sensitivity analysis.

Creating specification of a model can be challenging, which would explain why very few models have a specification. With small models, there is little need for these specifications; these types of models are generally not complex. For large models that will have a complexity, forgoing the specification increases the risk that the final model will not fulfill the needs of the model user and the model sponsor. The best way to view the specification is as blueprint for the model building.

Testing and Documenting Your Model

In this chapter, I will examine the process of testing models and providing user documentation for models. Without question, one of the most neglected stages of building models are the testing and documentation, because they are often performed toward the end of the modeling project and are subject to time constraints. I want to make sure that you have a firm understanding of why the testing and documentation should be considered just as important as any other stage in modeling.

Testing the Financial Model

You will notice that I have jumped into model testing before model building. Rest assured that this is deliberate, because the testing is planned around the model. There are no standard tests for financial models, but there are a series of test types that are used. Not all of these are appropriate for each model, and in order for the tester to understand which test types will be right for the model, the tester must first understand the model. The testing is never incidental; it doesn't just happen because the model has been built. It is a carefully planned and organized activity that has a significant part to play in the delivery of the model. Therefore, it is a critical part of the model design.

Why Test?

A best practice spreadsheet model should be reliable because decisions are likely to be made based upon the results and outputs that come from the model. This is only possible if the user has complete confidence in the model. It is impossible to guarantee that even a moderately complex model is an error-free model. Testing can, however, substantially reduce the risk of significant errors in a model.

▦ **Caution**   If testing is skipped or poorly handled, errors are likely to be discovered after the model has been put into use. There is nothing more damning than a model that has supposedly been tested but appears to be rife with errors. Errors at this stage can undermine the credibility of the model, the modeler, and the organization behind the model. Also keep in mind that the value of testing can be measured against the potential cost of a wrong decision. If a model is being used for an important and expensive business decision, the time and resources spent testing the model is time and money well spent. We have not yet discussed model audit, but it is important to know this distinction with testing. The model audit gives assurance that the model is what it says it is. In other words, if the requirement is ten-year cash flow model only, the model audit will sign off that the model is suitable for purpose. Testing, on the other hand, is about catching and minimizing the errors and verifying that the model works.

Who Should Test?

When testing a model, the objective is to demonstrate that the model does not work as it was intended. From this standpoint, the testing can focus on catching all the aspects in the model that are causing it to fail. It is impossible for modelers to be sufficiently critical of their own work; therefore, testing should always be carried out by an independent third party.

It is best for testing to be done by a team member who has been involved in other aspects of the overall project or aspects of the modeling other than the build stage. There are obvious benefits to using someone who is familiar with some of the issues that the model reflects. However, the technical skills required for a good tester are similar to those required for building the model. The tester should be able to understand and critique the detail of the formula and any code within the model.

When to Test?

When should testing commence? This is entirely based upon the program schedule. Testing, however, can only take place between the build and handover stages of the modeling life cycle. Under more pressing circumstances, it can be more difficult to identify the most appropriate time to test. Here are two examples:

- When there is great pressure for immediate results from the model, there is a trade-off to be made between gaining confidence in the model's results and trying to produce some reasonable answers quickly.

- When the model develops in a number of incremental stages, it is difficult to know when the time is right to first test the model, or when further changes are significant enough to require retesting.

There is no single correct answer for these questions, but there are points in time when testing should be considered. Generally, the testing period would commence just after the first version of the model is completed and run until all the errors are fixed and recommendations are implemented into the final model version. With very complex modeling projects, however, the modeler should consider implementing testing into the change control process. This way, testing will take place at regular intervals and after every major change in the model. This will be surplus to requirements for smaller models and can be costly. But with this approach, the model will always take into consideration any errors that are highlighted from testing.

Types of Tests

One of the unfortunate aspects of model testing is that there is no standard test. Instead, there are different types of tests that can be used, but not all of them are appropriate for every model. This dilemma of test choices is one reason why it is best for the tester to have spent some time with the modeler in order to gain an understanding of the model's structure and objectives. The next sections will provide brief summaries of the main model tests.

Numeric Tests

Numeric tests are used to determine if the outcome of an equation is in accordance with expected results by using an independent verification as a check. There are various ways to subject the results from a model to independent verification, including the following:

- It may be possible to reproduce some of the model results by hand or in a "quick and dirty" independent model.

- When the model is developed to replace a precursor model, any similarities or differences in common results can be explained by differing assumptions.

- When you know that there will not be time to test the model, ask two modelers to independently do the analysis and then compare their results.

A well-designed model will contain some internal numerical tests. A balanced balance sheet and consistency between calculated totals and subtotals are both necessary signs of a reliable model, but they are not proof that no errors still remain in the model. You will only get sensible results out of a model if you put realistic input assumptions in. While it is often outside the scope of the independent tester's work, the validity of the input assumptions will obviously affect the appropriateness of the answers.

Robustness Tests

The longer the expected life span of the model and the more different users of the model there will be, the more difficult the model test becomes. Instead of testing the validity of the model just under current circumstances, the tester needs to consider all the feasible circumstances that the model may be used for in the future. The two categories for robustness testing look at the environment that the model will operate in and the boundaries at which the model will potentially fail.

Environment Tests

Environment tests evaluate the operation of the model through several different computer configurations. Points to check include the hardware specification of the computer to be used, network and printer operations, and the specific versions of software being used. These tests will confirm that technical specification has not been exceeded, in particular the model size and calculation speed.

Boundary Tests

Boundary tests assess the behavior from the model when inputs reach sensible limits. For example, these tests would answer the following questions:

- How does the model cope with extremely large or extremely small inputs?

- Does typing in a zero produce division by zero errors?

If you type junk into a model, you expect to get junk out. But for many models, some form of data validation may be appropriate. Nevertheless, extreme cases of using particularly good or bad input assumptions are often important sets of model results, so the model should be able to cope with these.

Macro Tests

If the model contains macros, testing these can be extraordinarily time-consuming. Macros often only cause errors in a particular circumstance, which the tester will need to replicate to get an idea of how the error happens. The following issues are typical of the checks:

- Do the buttons, dialog boxes, and menus work appropriately?

- How does the macro cope with inappropriate data? How elegantly does it crash?

- If the macro involves file handling, what happens with duplicate or nonexistent files?

- Does the macro assume any default settings for the spreadsheet, such as sheet names, which a user may change?

- What happens when the user presses Escape during the macro execution?

When enough changes have been made in the model since the previous test, it makes material changes to the results possible. You need to consider how big a change to the results constitutes a material change and should then fall into the change control process.

Specification Tests

One of the objectives of the specification stage is to establish a common understanding of how the model should work. To achieve this objective, it is necessary to test that the specification agrees with the model sponsor's understanding of what the model will do. Clearly, this process does not require the model build to have been completed or even started.

Unique Formulas Tests

To test that the formulas in the model have been written correctly, check the model itself against the logical assumptions described in the model specification or in a similar document. A review of every unique formula in the model is an essential part of any thorough model test. Even so, the number of formulas in a reasonably large model makes this a daunting task.

I recommend resolving this problem by using the formula maps produced by a spreadsheet auditor package, such as OAK (by Operis) and Spreadsheet Professional (by Spreadsheet Innovations).

Common Types of Errors to Test

Fortunately, there are some errors in models that are very likely to occur, and an experienced tester will be able to quickly target those errors in the model. Once these errors have been corrected, the more unique errors can then be tackled. The next few sections will describe the more common errors.

Formulas Not Copied

With this error, a formula needs to be reflected either across a row or down a column, but it has somehow been missed and is not copied into all the required cells. There are several reasons how this would happen. In Chapter 2, the reasons why specific types of errors occur were discussed, such as the modeler talking on the phone while modeling. This type of error is quite difficult to locate, particularly if you have an erratic design for the model because a tester will be unable to be definite if the error is actually an error or if it is intended.

Wrong Reference

Nearly every formula in a spreadsheet refers back to another input or calculation. With the quantity of references in any large spreadsheet, it is inevitable that you will make mistakes and refer to the wrong cell (a pointing error). Sometimes, the resulting formula will produce a meaningless result, making it easy to spot with some simple numerical testing. If you are unlucky, the error in the result will be more subtle. While these types of errors are common, the testing should catch these quite easily. One way to alleviate these errors is to get into the habit of actually pointing to the cell that is being referenced rather than just naming it. Although this is a slower modeling process, it is more precise and mitigates the potential risk of using incorrect figures.

Sum Over the Wrong Range

A similar mistake is to include the wrong cell reference in a SUM formula. It is particularly easy to introduce this error when you insert an additional row in a block of cells that are being summed. If you insert a row in the middle of the block, the formula will automatically adjust to include the additional row. But if you insert a row immediately above or below the block, the new row will be omitted from the formula. This type of error should be picked up in the error checks built into the model.

Relative and Absolute References

Another commonly found error is caused by confusion between relative and absolute references. Remember that a cell reference in a formula of the form =D4 will change if you copy the formula across the row to E4, F4, and so on. Copied down a column, it will change to D5, D6, and so on. If you use the reference =$D$4, it will not change when copied across or down. You can also use semi-absolute references of the form $D4 or D$4.

The most common mistake is probably to use a relative reference instead of an absolute one. This is easy to spot numerically, but if you use an absolute reference in place of a relative one, it can be much more difficult to detect. The only way to find this mistake reliably is to use a formula map to go through all the unique formulas in the spreadsheet.

Unit Errors

Mixing up the appropriate unit for the elements in a calculation is another frequently occurring problem. Especially common is confusion between the order of magnitude for inputs, such as $s vs. $000s. This error should always be caught in testing. The modeler should be able to avoid making this type of error purely by making sure the units are clear and constant throughout the model.

Commonly Misused Functions

Certain functions are frequently used incorrectly. For instance, the most commonly misunderstood is the NPV function, used to calculate net present values.

The NPV function takes the form =NPV (rate, value1, value2, ...) where a rate is an appropriate discount rate and value1, value2, and so on are a stream of cash flows to be discounted. One common error in the NPV function is using an inappropriate discount rate, especially when the model contains calculations in a mixture of real and nominal prices.

A second common mistake concerns the timing of cash flows. By default, the NPV function assumes that all cash flows occur at the end of the time period you are considering. For an ongoing business, it is usually more appropriate to assume that cash flows occur in the middle of each time period. For a model based on annual time periods, using a discount rate of 10% and an end year rather than a midyear assumption decreases the present value calculated by 5%.

You can work through these problems by making an appropriate adjustment to the NPV function. Alternatively, it is often easier to calculate present values from first principle or use the Excel add-in function XNPV, which allows you to explicitly state the dates on which cash flows occur.

Other Functions That Often Cause Errors

Lookup and reference functions, such as VLOOKUP, HLOOKUP, INDEX, and MATCH, are susceptible to misuse, particularly when they return what may seem like an appropriate lookup instead of an error. This generally occurs when the range of the lookup reference is smaller than the true range, which means the lookup is working on a subset of the data. To avoid such mishaps, it is simpler to use a defined name (range name) to the data being referenced. That way, all the modeler needs to make sure is that they call the correct range name.

Using complex IF statements is a common issue for testing. The problem is magnified if there are embedded IF statements, which are notoriously difficult to decipher. Even when they have been detected, simplifying the formula is time consuming. Therefore, always test IF statements while they are being created. Even though there is a limit to how many IF statements (seven) can be embedded, still be sure to work well below this limit. If you are finding that you are using all seven IF statements in one formula, carefully consider your modeling technique as this is a clear sign of excessive complicated formula use.

Although these functions are often very useful, make sure that you understand exactly how they work before using them in your model. By making the formulas in your model easy to understand, you reduce the risk of introducing errors and increase the chances that a tester will find your mistakes.

The Test File

Testing is concerned with increasing confidence about the reliability of the model's results, so it is important that the testing process itself inspires confidence. A well-documented testing process will do just that. A test file is a useful document to illustrate how the model was tested and demonstrates that reasonable steps were taken to establish the accuracy of the model.

A test file should contain a record of the different tests that were carried out, such as annotated printouts of the model output and formula maps. The test file should also include an auditable trail of the errors found and corrections made and any other supporting documentation, such as the results of independent numerical tests.

Change Requests

An important part of the test documentation is a record of the changes recommended in the model and how they were implemented.

The tester completes the first section, which includes a description of the error found and, if appropriate, a suggested correction. The description should contain sufficient information for the modeler to correct most errors without having to spend time redoing the original test. The model builder takes the completed forms and makes the required changes, completing the second part of the form. I do not recommend that the tester make the changes to the model for the following reasons:

- The model builder usually understands the detail to the model better than anyone else. Change requests are sometimes the result from a misunderstanding by the tester rather than an actual error.

- When more than one person is working with the model at one time, it is important that a single copy is kept as the master version. The model builder can continue to work on the master version while testing is underway.

The third part of the form should be completed by the tester to check that the change has been made appropriately. Retesting changes is important because changes to a model, incorrectly made, can have knock-on effects in other parts of the model.

When going through the testing process, using a different version number for each batch of model changes will allow you to keep track of the effect of each correction. It will also make the test file clearer and the process easier to understand.

It can also be useful to classify requests on the change request form depending upon their importance:

- High priority for errors that materially change the results produced by the model

- Medium priority for errors that have a very small effect or may affect the results in the future

- Low priority for changes that are recommended to make the model easier to understand, but will not affect the results quoted

When time is limited, the builder can concentrate on high and medium priority changes and turn to low priority changes when time permits.

Points to Keep in Mind When Testing

The role of testing in modeling is not always appreciated, and it is important to ensure that models do get tested. The following points should be on your mind when building models.

- Testing can reduce the risk of significant errors appearing in your model results and build up the credibility and influence of the finished model.

- Errors discovered after the model has been put into use undermine the credibility of the modeler.

- Testing should always be done by someone other than the model builder, someone who is motivated to find mistakes in the model.

- If the model builder uses only one unique formula per row or column, it is much easier to test all the formulas in the model.

- Documenting the test process will help to build confidence in the finished model's results.

Providing Documentation in Models

The financial modeler should keep a log of all amendments made to the model to ensure a proper audit trail and documentation of changes made. A guide to using the financial model should also be developed to make certain that future users are able to become familiar with and use the model with ease.

Just as writing the specification often seems like a mission in complete boredom, writing the documentation can be very mundane. The unfortunate truth is there are far too few examples of documentation in financial modeling, possibly due to this boredom factor. Another reason why documentation is not completed or even commenced is due to timetables. For example, sometimes the point from beginning to handing over or implementing a model is very short, and there is barely enough time to even test the model. Finding the time to document a model under such circumstances may seem impossible.

Documentation, however, almost always needs to be done. The model that you develop could be responsible for helping to form decisions that have a significant financial impact on a project or an organization. Therefore, it is imperative that some details of how and why the model works accompany the model. Documentation is like the contents section in a study book; it puts into place where everything is located and how it all works together. Without it, you are blindly a trusting that the book will actually take you to where you want to go.

Good documentation is needed to ensure that the model is handled properly, even by users who were not involved throughout the development process. Ideally, your specification will serve as the basis for the user documentation. Remember that the better your specification, the more of it you can "recycle" in the final user guide.

The secret to documenting is to start as early as possible and keep on top of it each day. Avoid procrastinating because the longer it is left undone, the harder it will become to finish. During my model builds, I make sure the documentation is always performed at the end of each day and reviewed the following morning before carrying on with the model development. Another tip is to employ what I call "spot checks," whereby I choose a particular part of the model and check that there is documentation. I won't move on until that part is in place. Often I will nominate an independent party who will check through parts of the model and through the documentation to test if everything makes sense (not someone with the immediate modeling team but someone who is totally removed from the model build).

Documentation Structures

Consider that not all users of the model will be Excel "power users". If you know this will be the case, then it is imperative that there is some additional care placed on the documentation. For example, you will need to explain what a macro is before you explain what your macros does, and do the same for model checks before you explain how a user can go error-hunting.

Here is one way to organize the structure of your documentation:

Introduction

The first section of your documentation should explain the scope and the goal of the model. The user should understand what to use the model for and what to expect from it.

Assumptions and Inputs

Following the introduction, explain the structural assumptions and the relevant inputs. The user also needs to understand the interaction between the assumptions and the inputs. For instance, if any of the assumptions are subsequently changed during the modeling process, will the inputs automatically adjust to reflect this change, or will someone have to manually adjust the inputs?

Macro Handling

If the macros in the model are complex and require some user proficiency, include a section on handling macros. Depending on the client, this may even become technical with some code explanations. In simpler models with no (or automatic) macros, you may drop this section.

Outputs

One chapter should be dedicated to the output sheets. In this section, explain what the sheets show and how they should be read. This is also the section where you should include the definitions of the KPIs (key performance indicators).

Known Issues

Obviously, there should not be any issues with your model when it is final. Nonetheless, there may be points you will want to highlight to make sure that "user expectation" does not diverge too far from reality. Typical issues may include the following:

- Extreme elasticity effects: Your model may be accurate for certain input values, like a planned equity ratio anywhere from 5% to 95%, but may deliver wrong results for ratios of 0% or 100%. Known effects like that should be documented. Ideally, you should also explain the reason, for example, if this is due to a calculation simplification in order to increase usability of the model.

- Performance issues: Complex models may require a lot of processor power and memory, and recalculations and macros may take their time. Let the user know if this is the case. If applicable, give advice on how to improve the model's performance.

- Compatibility issues: It happens rarely but include in your documentation if you know your model has problems with certain versions of Excel (or Office), Windows, locale settings, and so forth.

Documentation Standards

Documentation is crucial to models. Irrespective of whether a model has it or not, every model should be documented. How that documentation occurs can be wrapped up by a generally accepted documentation standard.

Using Cell Comments

Cell comments are a way of communicating tips and instructions to users. When a user's cursor hovers over a commented cell, a text box appears displaying the message. To add a cell comment, right-click the cell you want to attach the comment to and choose Insert Comment. A yellow text box will appear with an arrow pointing to the activated cell. Type in your comment.

When you are finished, click on any other cell. The comment will be saved, attached to its anchor cell. The anchor cell will show a red triangle, indicating that a cell note is attached. (Note: The red triangle can be turned off by the Options dialog box, by choosing the Advanced option and scrolling down to Display.)

Tip When cell comments are shown, they sometimes hide the data behind them. You can move and resize the comment box by clicking directly on the box to activate it, then dragging the comment box to a new location. The comment's pointing arrow will stretch and remain attached to the comment's anchor.

If you have many comments in your worksheet, you might use the Reviewing toolbar to manage them. The toolbar appears when you choose Comments from the Review menu (to display all comments in Excel 2007/10/13, on the REVIEW tab, in the Comments group, click Show All Comments). Different buttons on the toolbar allow you to add comments, delete them, show all comments on the sheet, and tab from comment to comment.

By default, cell comments do not print when you print a worksheet. If you want comments to print, change the Comments setting in Page Setup. You have the choice of printing no comments, all comments at the bottom of the sheet, or as the comments appear directly on the sheet.

Note The comments must be displayed in the worksheet for them to print correctly. To display your comments on the sheet, choose the Show All Comments in the Comments group on the REVIEW tab.

Documentation Worksheets

Should you find that the instructions and explanations for a particular workbook are too unwieldy for cell comments, consider adding a separate worksheet in the workbook that contains only instructions and explanations. Give this worksheet tab a descriptive name, such as "InstructionsToUser" or "ModelnameDocumentation".

Note Notice that the suggested names for worksheets include no spaces between the words. This is a naming convention. If you are using hyperlinks and VBA, you will benefit by using this type of naming convention.

Excel's word processing capabilities are very limited, making editing of long text entries tedious. People often try to use Excel as a word processing tool, but that is just not in its bag of tricks. Don't fall into this habit as well. If you need to create considerable text documents in Excel, consider using MS Word and object linking the document to Excel. If you must use Excel, however, take these steps to make entering and editing long text passages easier:

- Format cells with the Wrap Text feature turned on. To activate this feature, on the HOME tab, in the Alignment group, click Wrap Text.

- Consider widening column A and using it for all entries.

- Always segment instruction topics into separate rows to minimize alignment problems when text is changed.

Thoughts About the Application to be Used

At some stage, the specifications will be locked down, and you will be in a position to begin developing the model. But first, put some thought into the application in which the model will be designed. Although you may already know you will be using Excel for modeling, consider that even with Excel there are different versions that can alter how you build the model. It is a safe assumption that your model will be developed in Excel 2003, Excel 2007/10, or Excel 2013. The essential modeling is the same throughout; however, the ease of development becomes more apparent in the later versions. (I would strongly advise those who are still using excel 2003 to make the switch to a later version.)

Spreadsheet packages are good at numerical manipulation and have a wide range of financial and mathematical functions. It is easy to present calculations in a readable form and to mix text and graphical display. Spreadsheets are enormously popular, widely available, and easy to use.

The flexibility of spreadsheets makes it possible to use them to tackle problems that would be more appropriately modeled with different software. Their availability and ease of use makes this an extremely common mistake. Therefore, before you design a spreadsheet, make sure that a spreadsheet is the most appropriate tool for the job.

Excel 2010/13 has a wide range of add-in functions that allows you to do numerous unusual calculations. Many of these can be very useful, but if you find that you are using them often, you would probably be better off using a specialist package. For example, if you are using a lot of the database functions, a database application such as Microsoft Access may be the better option.

This chapter is an augmentation to the planning of the modeling process. When working on medium to large models, there is so much that can be gained from having a plan with all the stages clearly established. I have come across completed large commercial models where there has been no documentation whatsoever. In my opinion, these models are not complete if they lack documentation. In the case of testing, although it irks me to say it, it is possible to complete a model without going through testing. Much depends on how that model will be used. For instance, testing may not be necessary if the model will be used to calculate the break-even point of an investment.

On the other hand, if a model is calculating how much funding from financial institutions and investors will be required to push a company through some turbulent times, then clearly a tested model is a must.

6

Designing and Building Your Model

The design of the model is all about ensuring that the physical model will work once it is built and will actually function in the manner that is expected in the planning.

How the model is designed will be influenced by the ability of the modeler to translate requirements of the model sponsor into a methodical modeling project. This means prior to designing the model, the modeler must look at aspects such as:

- The impact of the requirements on the three key modeling concepts: inputs, calculations, and outputs.

- The intended use of the model. This will determine if it will be a deterministic-type model (a deterministic model is one that, given a fixed set of inputs, always produces the outputs), or a stochastic model, which means the modeler must consider the effects of probabilities on the outputs.

- The time scales of the model. Is this a time-value model or one that represents a specific moment only?

- The dependency of the model on external data such as databases and ERP (Enterprise Resource Management) systems.

- The potential size of the model, which is usually based on how much data the model is expected to hold.

- The project time scale, which will allow the modeler to assess whether building the model is realistic.

- The complexity of the modeling project. The model will generally reflect the environment that it is built in; a complex environment is likely to require a complex model.

Don't be tempted to start building the model too soon, especially when you are under pressure to produce results from the model quickly. Taking time to complete the design is well worth it, because it will allow the modeler to manage any complexities all during the design rather than when building. You will also enjoy the following results:

- The model is quicker and easier to build because you have a model specification that describes what the model will do rather than having to work it out as you go along.

- The model is less prone to errors if you have a written description of how the model works.

- The model is less likely to have to be reworked if you have taken some time to build a common understanding of the requirement of the model. To have such an understanding will mean the design should be preceded by a project scope document that has been jointly agreed upon by the model sponsor and the modeler.

Managing Complexity

There are several books that cover writing error-free software, none better than *Code Complete* (second edition) by Steve McConnell (Microsoft Press, 2004). McConnell states that the most important problem is managing complexity, which is a problem with financial modeling simply because Excel's versatility comes at price. Excel models tend to become complex quickly and easily. One of the reasons why so many Excel models become far too complex is that there are literally so many facets to Excel. With so many functions, codes, and utilities, there are just too many that are not matched by a user's knowledge.

If asked to rate their ability, many Excel users would claim to be far higher than an independent experienced Excel practitioner would. In other words, most believe that their skills in Excel are more than adequate, and why? One reason may be because Excel does not impose any intrinsic methodologies and structures on the user. For example, if you look at a complex model, you would only see one formula at a time and it may refer to cells and sheets you cannot see. What you can see is (often) a sea of numbers, which creates visual clutter. What this means is that users are not always aware of what is really going on outside of the cell they are working in. And because there are few alerts given by the application, users will actually believe that once a formula has been created everything is okay. Herein lies the problem—this is not necessarily the case.

As a result, it is possible to use some of the functions erroneously without really understanding their full impact until quite late in the modeling process when those errors start to appear. Most modelers at this stage would plough on regardless, firefighting any problems as they arise. Unfortunately, the result would be a finished model that is really a hodgepodge of functions, hard-coded adjustments, and dead links that has gone some way off the original route.

To put it bluntly, the reality is that of the 120 models I have reviewed in a four-year period, there were less than 12 that I would class as models that show any sense of planning and design to warrant being called financial models. This may be just a coincidence, but clearly there is a problem that needs to be addressed with the way models are being built.

Figure 6-1 presents a high-level design model of medium complexity in a flow diagram. You can clearly see that the model will be made up of several items or modules, such as the time-related inputs, the workings (calculations), and the reports. These modules have been classed into categories, for instance, inputs, calculations, or outputs. Notice the addition of the category called "Admin." This topic will be covered later in Chapter 14 when I discuss modeling in a way that gives the users transparency.

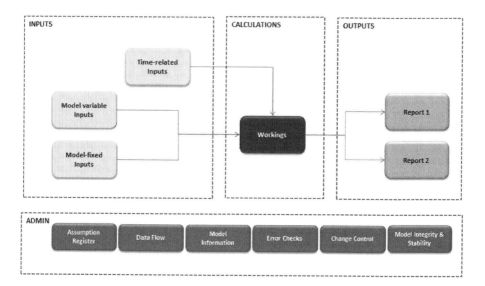

Figure 6-1. A high-level diagram of the model components is shown here

By creating such a diagram, you can start to see how these modules (which are essentially worksheets) will link to each other, and you can begin to make a map of the entire model.

You can consider the data flow and links between the modules in the high-level diagram by creating a data-flow table. The data-flow table is useful as a control mechanism for the data and links, and it also serves as a checklist of the data during the model building. A sample of a data-flow table can be seen in Figure 6-2.

Worksheet (Module)	Type	Specifications Approved?	Has Formula?	User Interaction
Model variable Inputs	Inputs	Yes	None	Full
Model-fixed Inputs	Inputs	Pending	None	Full
Time-related Inputs	Inputs	Not required	Yes	None
Workings	Calculations	Not required	Yes	None
Report 1	Outputs	Yes	Yes	Partial
Report 2	Outputs	Yes	Yes	Partial
Assumption register	Admin	Not required	Yes	None
Data Flow	Admin	Not required	None	None
Model Information	Admin	Not required	None	None
Error Checks	Admin	Not required	Yes	None
Change Control	Admin	Not required	Yes	None
Model Integrity and Stability	Admin	Not required	Yes	None

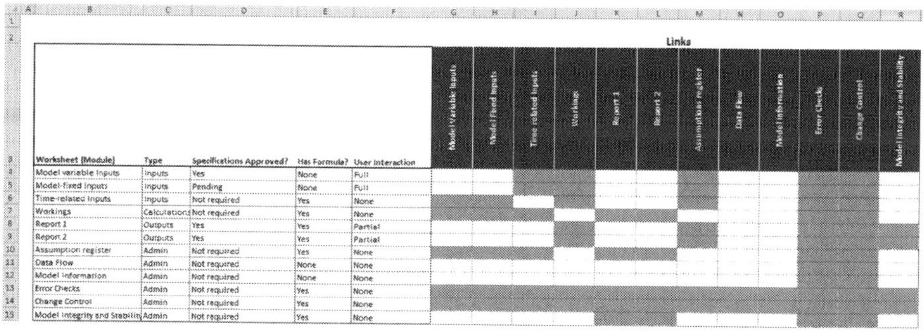

Figure 6-2. A table with the data flows in the impending model serves as useful control for the modeler

The next part to the design is to explore each of these modules and decide the layouts, the look and feel, and the information that they will hold. This may mean you will start by developing a template that will be the standard template for all the modules in the model.

Figure 6-3 is a snapshot of the model-fixed inputs template. Notice that each individual section is clearly labeled; also there is an unused column in column A. This column will be used to provide references to the assumptions.

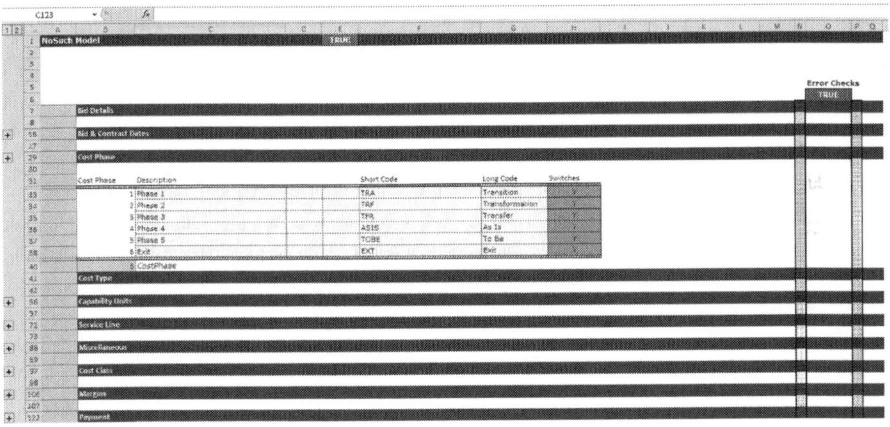

Figure 6-3. This is a sample of the model-fixed inputs template which contains the non-variable inputs to the model

During the design of all the worksheets, it will be important that the physical file size of the full model is considered. In addition, make sure that the specifications clearly indicate who will be the model owner and describe what exactly the model will be and which application it will be built in. Even though it may be clear to the modeler that the application will be Excel, this should still be stated in the specification to establish a clear understanding between the model sponsor and the modeler. There should also be some mention of the acceptable speed of processing. In the design, the modeler must be careful to keep these specifications in sight. With numerous worksheets in a model, each with numerous calculations, more computer processing power is required. Remember that it is simply not good enough to deliver a model to the model user. Even though the model may function, it may be so large and so processor-intensive that it takes minutes rather than seconds to perform any calculations.

▓ **Tip**   What is the optimum Excel file size? The answer is that "it depends." No two workstations have uniform performance compared to one another. Another point to consider is what the model user will tolerate. Excel version 2007 and later versions have a more efficient file system; therefore, models developed with these versions are considerably smaller and more compact than those developed in older versions. I have my own hard-and-fast rules that I use to discipline myself when developing client models. I never exceed 0.5 megabytes per worksheet within the model. If I have a model with ten worksheets, it will be less than five megabytes. Again, this is my rule and it works for me, but it's a good idea to come up with your own working rule to the file size.

Building Your Model

At this stage, you should be clear about the model's design; have an understanding of the inputs, calculations and the outputs; and have in hand an approved scope and specification of the model. Now it is time to begin actually building the model. In this section, I will discuss the intricacies of the model build and how to best approach it.

Define the Modeling Tool(s) for the Job

When performing financial modeling using Excel, it is first important to establish whether Excel as your only tool of choice. In such situations where there is a heavy reliance on data, I do use Microsoft Access in combination with Excel. In these cases, Access handles all the data and becomes the back end of the model and Excel handles the calculations and outputs and becomes the front end. However, handing over such a model can be fraught with problems. Some quirks with Access and how it works with Excel that are not problematic on your computer may crop up on the user's computer. One way to avoid this problem is to create an application so that the entire model becomes an executable program, irrespective of whether it is part of Access or Excel. That is, however, beyond this book. I bring it up because occasionally as a modeler you may need to consider using Access. However, for the purposes of this book, the tool of choice will only be Excel.

Have a Clear Approach

There are two approaches to building models: the top-down method (see Figure 6-4) and the bottom-up method (see Figure 6-5). I endorse the top-down approach because the other method can cause even the most seasoned modeler to make errors.

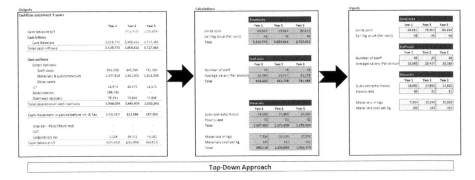

Figure 6-4. The top-down approach starts with the outputs

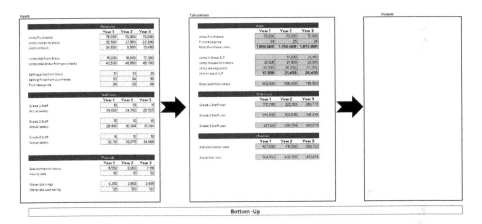

Figure 6-5. The bottom-up approach starts from the detail inputs and calculations, but the outputs are not used as the target

With the bottom-up method, the real problem is that this approach is focused on collecting data and how that data can be manipulated with calculations. This is the main priority and therefore this approach ignores the overall structure of the model. In other words, it works at the detail end of modeling first and puts the comprehensive presentation last. The problems start to appear once the modeler is in the development stage, because inevitably issues begin to emerge that weren't foreseen and planned. As a result, the modeler now has some major reworking to do. Due to this unstructured approach, the modeler is most likely going to create errors along the way because the modeling is based on "as you see it" type thinking.

Telltale signs of models built in this manner can be observed in the way that parts in the model just don't seem to relate together. For example, often it is unclear exactly what each part from the model is doing and even if some of the parts are really necessary. The model then becomes more a showcase of the individual modeler's changeable thought processes in each stage of the model and so lacks any real coherence or consistency.

Let's contrast this approach with the top-down approach by going through this example:

A model that will have a cash flow forecast for the next three years and should also have actual cash for the previous year.

How would you go about building this model? First, take a look at what you need to produce, which is a cash flow statement. Even though it was not required, you will need to create a profit and loss statement in order to look at revenues and costs. It's also clear that the model will need to accommodate some data inputs from users of the model, so they can punch in the previous year's actuals. Again, even though it hasn't been asked for, you will also need to build in some sensitivity, which means including a separate area for the user to flex the model inputs.

This top-down approach means that you are looking at the wider model and beginning to think about how the components will fit together. You are also defining the boundaries and subsequently working at the bottom in contrast to having no boundaries and working at the top. My advice is to work from top to the bottom by starting the model build with the outputs. Think in terms of the reports the sponsor and model users require and then work back into the inputs. That way, you will fit the inputs and calculations to the outputs, in contrast to a bottom-up method, where the outputs will not be known until the end of the model build. In this case, you will end up with far too many inputs and calculations.

Get Approval of the Outputs

The outputs that will be the reports and statements should always be the modeler's primary goal because they are the reason for the model build. Within the specification, you should have established the exact outputs. In most instances, the sponsor will have a clear idea of what is needed, such as financial statements (profit and loss, balance sheets, or cash flow statements) or budgets. It could even be a mix of these outputs and also include a number of financial valuations and financial metrics.

Crucially the modeler will need to make sure these outputs are not only clear but are approved and signed off by the sponsor. The best way to achieve this is to create physical samples of these outputs without any financial data that can be presented to the sponsor. Then the sponsor can make any adjustments and amendments and give final approval of the samples. Once the outputs are locked down, the process of building the model becomes defined and the final goals are clear and set. Often organizations will have standard templates or may require that any outputs have a particular layout and feel to them, so the modeler should also make sure that the model outputs are in line with the model user's requirements.

Time Scales

When building the model, it's inevitable that you will need to establish some method of working with time periods, which can be years, quarters, months, weeks, and even days. The trick is how to get the model to relate to moving periods, for instance, a change from reporting in years to reporting in quarters and then annually after the first year. In addition, the model needs to also have the ability to handle variations in dates, such as changes in specific dates like project milestone dates, project start dates, or even changes in payment terms for different suppliers. This aspect of modeling presents major problems for modelers and as a result leads to shortcuts being taken, which later will prove to be counterproductive.

The key is to build the model with the smallest time periods that could be effectively used. Don't get concerned if the specification asks for reports to be in years. The actuality is that to get to those years you need to have the months, so build the model based on months. If you happen to ignore this facet, you will eventually end up regretting it.

Here is an example. You have been asked by the sponsor to build a model that gives cash flow forecasts for three years. You happily build a model that is based in years ignoring the months. Further down the line, you discover that, in fact, the model users will require the ability to process sensitivity analysis that allows them to see what would happen if they change their creditor payment terms from 30 days, 45 days, 60 days, or 90 days. This small adjustment will have a big impact on your model, and you will be forced to rebuild it because the effect of these period changes will affect all the date-reliant calculations on the model.

The solution to this time issue is to create a template in the model that has the smallest time periods (such as months) to the largest (such as years) and subsequently be synchronized as in Figure 6-6. This allows the modeler to refer to this template for any dates and time periods and then use lookups to see when that date occurs within the time periods.

	From	To	Period	Period Number	Phase	Year	Month in Year	Calendar Month Number	Month Name	Timeline	Quarter	Active Month Flag	Active Month Countdown	Company Year	Company Month	Annual Summary

Months

From	01-Aug-2005	01-Sep-2005	01-Oct-2005	01-Nov-2005	01-Dec-2005	01-Jan-2006	01-Feb-2006	01-Mar-2006
To	31-Aug-2005	30-Sep-2005	31-Oct-2005	30-Nov-2005	31-Dec-2005	31-Jan-2006	28-Feb-2006	31-Mar-2006
Period	1	2	3	4	5	6	7	8
Period Number	-5	-4	-3	-2	-1	1	2	3
Phase								
Year	0	0	0	0	0	1	1	1
Month in Year	7	8	9	10	11	1	1	1
Calendar Month Number	8	9	10	11	12	1	2	3
Month Name	August	September	October	November	December	January	February	March
Timeline	M-5	M-4	M-3	M-2	M-1	Y1M1	Y1M1	Y1M1
Quarter	Pre	Pre	Pre	Pre	Pre	Q1	Q1	Q1
Active Month Flag	1	1	1	1	1	1	1	1
Active Month Countdown	149	148	147	146	145	144	143	142
Company Year	2005/6	2005/6	2005/6	2005/6	2005/6	2005/6	2005/6	2005/6
Company Month	5	6	7	8	9	10	11	12
Annual Summary	Year 0	Year 0	Year 0	Year 0	Year 0	Year 1	Year 1	Year 1

Annual

Year	Year 0	Year 1	Year 2	Year 3	Year 4	Year 5	Year 6	Year 7
From	01-Aug-2005	01-Jan-2006	01-Jan-2007	01-Jan-2008	01-Jan-2009	01-Jan-2010	01-Jan-2011	01-Jan-2012
To	31-Dec-2005	31-Dec-2006	31-Dec-2007	31-Dec-2008	31-Dec-2009	31-Dec-2010	31-Dec-2011	31-Dec-2012
Company Year	2005/6	2005/6	2006/7	2007/8	2008/9	2009/0	2010/1	2011/2
Months	5	12	12	12	12	12	12	12
Active Months	0	0	0	0	0	0	0	0

Qtr

Quarter Number	1	2	3	4	5	6	7	8
From	01-Aug-2005	01-Jan-2006	01-Apr-2006	01-Jul-2006	01-Oct-2006	01-Jan-2007	01-Apr-2007	01-Jul-2007
To	31-Dec-2005	31-Mar-2006	30-Jun-2006	30-Sep-2006	31-Dec-2006	31-Mar-2007	30-Jun-2007	30-Sep-2007
Months	5	3	3	3	3	3	3	3
Quarter Label	Pre	Q2	Q3	Q4	Q5	Q6	Q7	Q8
Check	2,984,033							

END

Figure 6-6. The time-scale template is used to control the model time values by calculating all the different time periods that could be used in the model

For instance, using our example about the cash flow and change in creditor payment date, we could still produce a yearly cash flow for the users. However, when they made their change request, we could use the time-scale template in Figure 6-6 to state the number of days. This time scale would then work out when in the year 30 days, 45 days, or 60 days occur in the cash flow.

Developing Styles and Templates

Using colors in a model can be very helpful for the users. There is a general idiom that you should avoid creating worksheets with several colors for a number of reasons, one being that it's distracting. However, I firmly endorse the use of colors in financial modeling so long as they are consistent and practical. By creating a model style using colors, you can distinguish between the types of information and also alert the user to how the model is processing the information. For instance, you could use a pale yellow to alert the user that this is an input field and use a grey color to signify that a cell has a function or link. This way, the user will not be required to do anything but observe.

Choose your own color styles but make them distinctive and also themed. For example, if you use a pale yellow to designate an input cell, you could also use a pale yellow with a green border to designate an input cell that has a drop-down list. This way, the users will know that inputs are always a pale yellow but you still have the option of distinguishing between types of inputs.

Figure 6-7 gives a sample of a style sheet. This should be provided within the model to act as a legend and to inform the user of the color conventions being used. Look closely at the top of the worksheet in Figure 6-7. Notice that this style sheet is also incorporating the template format that will be used throughout the model as in Figure 6-8.

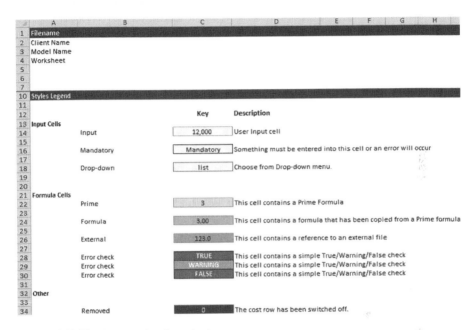

Figure 6-7. This is a sample of a style sheet

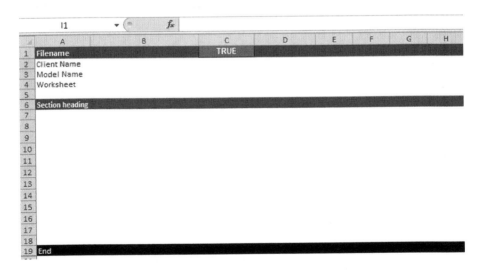

Figure 6-8. This shows the worksheet template format

Define the Structure of the Workbook

Each workbook should have a broad set of rules that are consistent across all the worksheets in the model. The modeler should establish these rules at the start of the model build and maintain them throughout the model. For instance, column A could be left blank on all worksheets. (I leave this blank as I can then use it for documentation and assumption references before closing the model.) The other most important feature is to keep all data within the same structure of columns. For example, if Year 1 starts in column D and Year 2 in column E, this should be replicated across the entire model in the inputs, calculations, and outputs. By using a consistent structure, there are definite benefits for reducing the risk of errors, such as pointing errors.

Working with the Inputs

The inputs should be kept distinct from any other model information. I choose to always keep the inputs on a different worksheet, and if there are unlike data types for inputs also separate these onto different worksheets. A sample input worksheet is presented in Figure 6-9. Notice that the format and style are consistent through each model and that the inputs are distinguished from the calculations by using colors.

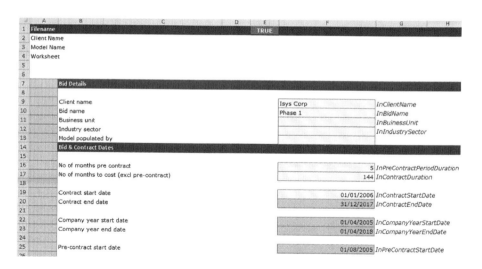

Figure 6-9. With this inputs worksheet, notice that the format and styles are now consistent

Figure 6-10 is different because the data is time-based. Therefore, a separate worksheet has been used, but the style still remains the same.

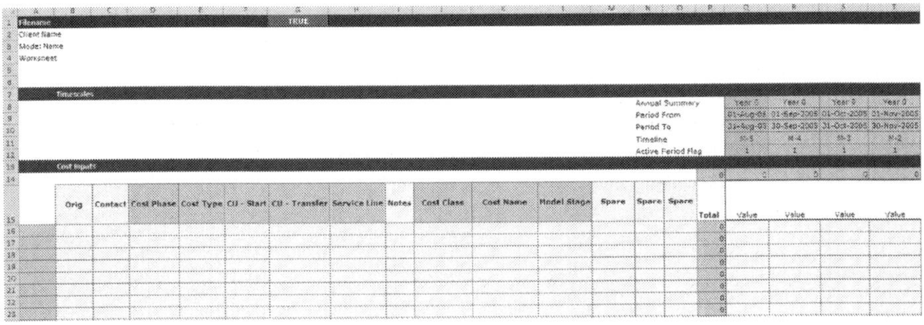

Figure 6-10. This figure shows a time-based inputs worksheet

Working with the Calculations

What do I mean by the term "calculations"? Well, in their simplest form, calculations are the formulas that are used on the inputs to create the outputs. They are also the methods that are used to bring functionality into the model and make up the process of translating information into something tangible for the model owner or sponsor. I want to get these points across because the calculations are often seen as just a set of formulas. From my experience, little attention is given to them from anyone but the modeler.

The calculations performed on the model are without a doubt the most critical element to any model. It is here where the modeler's interpretation and understanding about the process, or business, is clearly demonstrated. Frankly, anyone who is looking at a model will gain some valuable insight into the inner workings of the model by taking a look at the calculations. The reason so many users of models are put off by the calculations is more due to the aesthetics of the calculations rather than the actual calculations themselves. There can be nothing more frustrating than having a jumble of formulas staring at you with numerous levels of links all throughout the model.

Therefore, it is vitally important that calculations have these characteristics: structured with a consistent layout, follows best practice by not having a long or too complex formula, and maintains row consistency.

First, consistently try to put your calculations into one worksheet as much as possible. Even if it means that it will be a long worksheet, you can invariably create categories and keep a neat structure. There is a good reason behind having just one worksheet. Calculations that are developed on several worksheets will lead the modeler into creating a myriad of links from one worksheet to another, which will be terribly difficult to follow. It's very easy to then lose control and introduce duplication errors as another formula or link is created to do exactly the same job simply because you have lost track of what all the links are doing. By employing just one calculation worksheet, any issues with links and errors will clearly be coming from just that one worksheet.

Something else to keep in mind is that there should never be any hard-coded numbers or static hard-coded numbers within the calculations. After all, they are calculations. It really does dismay me when I find a modeler has placed a static hard-coded number right in the middle of a row of formula. It just brings in a suspicion about the credibility of the modeler and if there is a possible fudge factor coming to play.

Note Fudge factor is a term used to describe a random or ad hoc number that has been introduced into an otherwise logical model in order to induce a specific result.

If you have to use some fudge factor, my advice is to not place it into the calculations as a hard-coding. Instead, add it to the assumptions and create an input in the input worksheet and document the reasoning for this factor. Now you can introduce this input into the calculations, but at least there is some reference as to why it's being used.

In Figure 6-11, although I have not used any type of expansive functions, the calculations are in one worksheet shown in their categories. You can clearly see the link to the input and the subsequent calculation. The modeler should be aiming to maintain a structure that follows the inputs so that it's easy to keep up with where the link comes from and how the calculation has been put together. It is also good practice to bring the actual input into the calculation worksheet as a link and then make the calculation from that worksheet and not directly from the inputs.

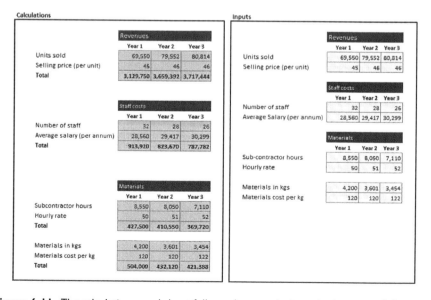

Figure 6-11. The calculations worksheet follows the same logic as the inputs worksheet

In Figure 6-12, the calculations are made directly from the inputs (sometimes referred to as a three-dimensional formula). Although this is still a viable way to model, it is clearly a lot more difficult to trace the calculations. Imagine that there are hundreds of inputs and calculations, and there are some errors that need to be corrected. The method of finding them will now require switching between the inputs and the calculations; a switch that could be compounded if there are also numerous calculation worksheets. Although it seems like duplication bringing the inputs into the calculation worksheet and making the calculations in that worksheet, it is cleaner and more sensible modeling. Once you develop this method of working, it will become second nature.

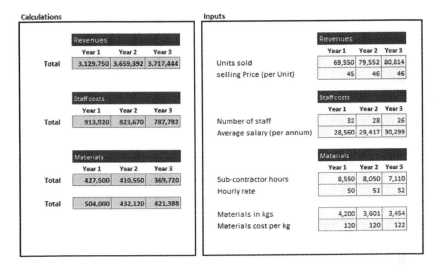

Figure 6-12. There are no links to the inputs; the calculations are made on the inputs directly

Working with the Outputs

The outputs will be governed by the approval from the sponsor and model users; therefore, it is likely they will need to conform to a specific layout and format. Even with this in mind, there should still be consistency. For instance, no matter what type of outputs (reports) are required, these should link to the calculations worksheet. In other words, do not make the mistake of linking the outputs to inputs—this is a characteristic of a model that has not been well thought out. By linking to the calculation worksheet, the flow of information will run from the inputs to the calculation to the outputs; therefore, any problems in the outputs can be traced to the calculations, then to the inputs and corrected.

If the modeler breaks this flow and makes some direct links to the inputs, thus bypassing the calculations, there is a strong likelihood that the following will happen:

- Any changes that are made in the outputs that require some conversion with calculation before they can be presented will be circumvented. The output will now be different than the calculation worksheet (see Figure 6-13).

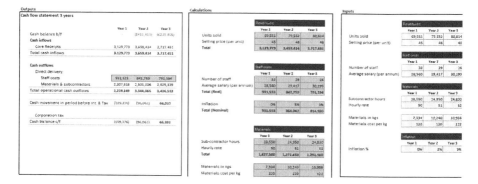

Figure 6-13. The staff costs in the outputs do not match the staff costs in the calculations worksheet because they have come from the inputs worksheet

- There is a strong likelihood of having split variables. For instance, the cost of sales in the profit and loss output could be coming from the inputs, and the cost of sales in the cash flow output could be coming from the calculations.

- It will be difficult to create adequate error checks that can signify a problem because the checks will have two sources. How will you determine which one is correct?

Recap

The model build will consist of a number of principles and actions. Here is what has been discussed so far in this chapter:

- Think about which tools you will be using or require for the project.

- Set yourself up for a top-down approach as opposed to a bottom-up approach.

- Make sure the outputs have been approved by the sponsor and model user and then close off.

- Develop a time scale template with the lowest time periods to the highest.

- Develop a consistent worksheet template for the entire model.

- Create a modeling style and format and put these into a legend template.

- Work according to a defined structure for all the workbooks.

- Create the inputs in one workbook but make a separate workbook for calculations and outputs.

- Use the calculations and bring all inputs into the calculations. Do not use hard-coded numbers or fudge factors in the calculations.

- Worksheets should have a flowing link. Calculations are linked to inputs and outputs are linked to calculations. Avoid hopping from outputs to inputs.

Planning for Errors

In Chapter 2, the theory and the reality of errors was covered thoroughly, so in this section I will discuss how to deal with the knowledge that errors are a symptom of financial modeling. Planning for errors means dealing with them, and this is more about the modeler's mindset. The modeler needs to think about "what is it that made this error?" and then think further about what can actually happen. In other words, the modeler needs to be a couple of steps ahead of the model user in order to foresee the potential errors that can occur.

For instance, an error may occur within a cell that has totals in it because the users may choose to overwrite the formula and put in place a different function that they feel is more suitable. Whether the model user has the right to do this is beside the point; the simple fact is that an error occurs because a calculation cell has been tampered with. The crucial aspect here is this: has the modeler foreseen this possibility and added some sort of error checking?

Creating the Error Template

The modeler should create an error worksheet that collects all the errors in the models on a worksheet-by-worksheet basis. What this means is that each worksheet can contain its own error checks, which are subsequently collected as a group check on the worksheet. After that, the group check is collected by the error checking template.

In Figure 6-14, the error check is shown, and it shows the group check from seven worksheets. The error check template then shows the status of all seven worksheets. Notice the time inputs worksheet has returned an error. By looking at this template, the user will know that there is a problem in that one worksheet.

Figure 6-14. An error check template is shown here

In Figure 6-15, the time inputs worksheet has an error in one of the staff cost lines. The modeler has anticipated that if any of the detail columns are blank, then an error will occur; this is the error that is collected in the error template. The top of the worksheet shows the group error taken from column U, which now signifies that this entire worksheet is in error and will need fixing. The error cell in E1 is then linked to the worksheet named error check.

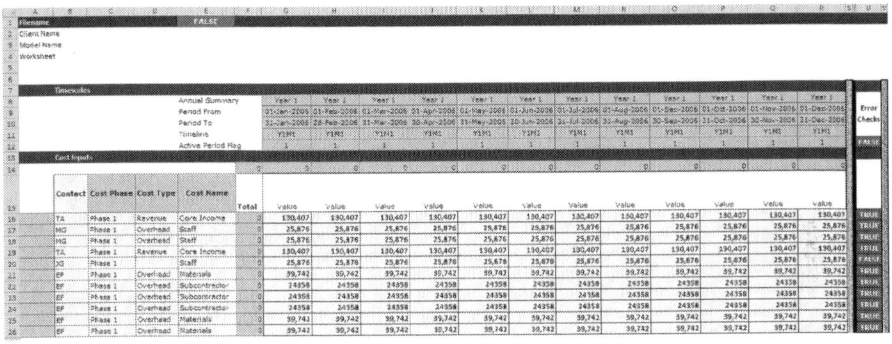

Figure 6-15. The time inputs worksheet with data is shown here. Notice that there is an error because something is missing

Displaying the Errors

There is no standard method of displaying errors. The method I use is visual as well as providing a message—either "False," "Warning," or "True." The message "False" means that a significant issue is apparent and needs to be rectified as it has an effect on the model. The "Warning" message is little used, but I use it to signal that there is an issue although it will not have any detrimental effect on the model. For example, "Warning" would appear where the user has input a number that is exactly the same as another number that has already been inputted. This would just be a warning to check that this is intentional. "True" signifies there are no issues and therefore no error has occurred. However, do not feel that you should use the same messages as I use, for instance, you could use "OK," "Investigate," and "Error" instead.

Creating and formatting the error message is a two-stage process. First, select a cell and on the Home tab and in the Number group, click the Dialog Box Launcher. Use the Custom Number format and in the Type textbox type "FALSE";"WARNING";"ERROR" or any combination that you wish to use (see Figure 6-16).

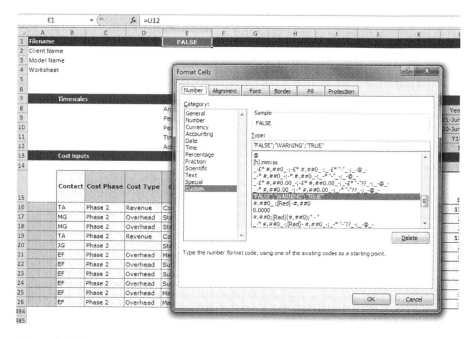

Figure 6-16. The error checks can be created through the format menu

Next, apply conditional formatting for each of the three conditions to the same cell, starting with ERROR. On the Home tab, in the Styles group, click Conditional Formatting and then click New Rule. Choose Format only cells that contain, as shown in Figure 6-17.

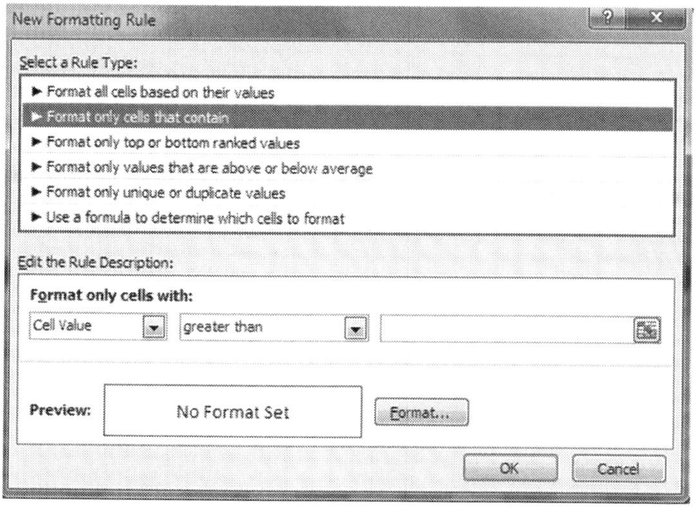

Figure 6-17. The conditional formatting with a new rule is shown here

There are three conditions that must be set. First, ensure that Cell Value is displayed in the first drop-down under Edit the Rule Description. Click the next drop-down arrow and select greater than. Click in the last box on the right and enter the number 1. Now format the condition with a red fill. Click the Format button, then the Fill tab, then the Color arrow, and then click Red (see Figure 6-18).

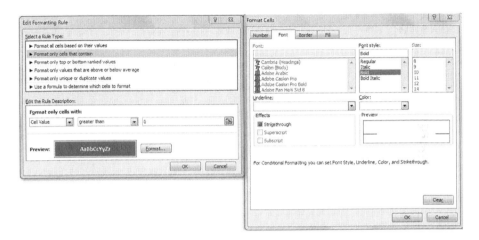

Figure 6-18. Use the fill color to set the condition

Make sure you also set the font and font style (on the Font tab) to the preference that you require. Click OK when you are finished. Now, apply two more conditions: one for WARNING and one for TRUE. For WARNING, use the less than 0 condition with a fill color of orange. For the last condition, TRUE, set the rule description to equal to 0 and use the green fill color.

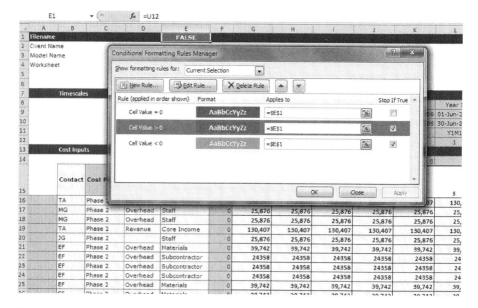

Figure 6-19. Establishing the conditional formatting for all three error conditions is shown here

Now, there are only two steps left for the modeler: determine which parts to the model require error checks and what exactly the checks should be testing.

Case Study: Planning a Financial Model

In this case study, we will be planning an actual model from the feasibility to scoping and then getting the specification, putting together the model design, and finally creating a testing specification. We are not going to go through the model build, so the assumption will be that the model is built. This case study is focused on how to mount a feasibility study for a model build. The reason I have used this example is that the feasibility is the start of any modeling. It is a crucial piece for financial modeling because it will dictate whether the model build will continue or not. It is imperative that you understand the basics of building a good feasibility study to present to the sponsor or customer.

The Brief

The newly appointed vice president of financial analysis and metrics for Nonsuch Corporation is dissatisfied with the level of financial information available to the organization. The organization is going through a two-year transformation program to change the way it delivers services to clients, and the availability of up-to-the-minute and accurate financial information is critical to the VP's decision-making.

The VP has brought in a financial modeling firm to produce a feasibility study for the company on the strength of their financial information and provide any options on how to improve on the weaknesses.

About the Feasibility Study

The process of conducting a feasibility study can be quite lengthy, although the document or findings will be reasonably short and concise. A feasibility study is a document that identifies each of the solution options available and rates the likelihood of each option achieving the desired result. It should include the following parts:

- A description of the business problem (the modeling project)
- A list of the requirements for a solution to fix the problem (or realize the opportunity)
- Available options for delivering a solution
- An assessment of the feasibility of each option
- A list of the risks and/or issues associated with each option
- A preferred option to be approved for implementation

This feasibility assessment will be undertaken by the financial modeler and presented to the model sponsor.

For our case study, the assumption is that the business case for the project will have been completed previously, and therefore completion of this feasibility will add more rigor to the solution options presented in the business case.

The main purpose of the feasibility study is to ascertain the likelihood of each solution option identified for meeting the stated business requirements. Although the risks, issues, and constraints are important, the project is less likely to be a success if the solution option chosen is unlikely to be feasibly implemented.

To determine the likely feasibility of an option, a range of "assessment" methods are undertaken. As there are a myriad of potential methods attainable to assess feasibility, I suggest you take time to consider the most appropriate method available in your project. The outcome of the feasibility study is the confirmed solution option for inclusion within the business case. The next stage, after the solution option has been approved, is to define the project scope and structure within the project's terms of reference document (a statement of the objectives and purpose of the project).

The Assessment

As we work through this case study, let's call this project the financial tool feasibility (FTF). Now let's break down the feasibility study into its components to be presented to the VP of financial analysis and metrics.

Problem Statement

When conducting a feasibility assessment or study, it is very likely that some issues will arise during the assessment. These issues should be collected during the study and then listed in priority from the most to the least severe.

Business Environment

Any successful organization requires timely and up-to-the-minute financial information to support decision-making and to forecast the future. Nonsuch Corporation has either lost or has not had the mechanism in place to deliver financial information that can be quickly and easily outputted to senior staff. Due to the demand of the transformation program, there is now a serious requirement that this financial information be available to the VP of financial analysis and metrics.

Business Vision

The corporation is looking to redefine how it interacts with its customers and clients in the next two years as a step toward achieving higher growth and profit maximization for the future.

Business Units

The current business unit relevant for this project is the financial analysis and metrics departments, which are part of the wider finance department.

Business Location

This is a global business with locations across several countries and regions. This feasibility study is for the group vice president and is therefore relevant for every location.

Business Information

There is a need to understand the repositories, databases, and enterprise resource systems (ERPs) available in the organization, which once the due diligence has commenced will result in a data flow diagram.

Business Technologies

The list of the existing business technologies that are relevant for this project (like network attached storage or data servers) is not available until the completion of the due diligence. Once the details are provided, a description for each major technology together with a technology architecture diagram to highlight the interfaces between current business technologies will be placed in this section.

Business Problem

The business problem is a lack of visibility of the key financials of the business and therefore no transparency.

The reasons why this problem exists are currently unknown but could be due to the lack of historical investment in the financial systems and infrastructure. This problem is having a major negative impact on the organization's response to its market. It is envisaged that the problem will need to be resolved quite rapidly as the transformation of the entire organization (not just the finance department) will be two years from start to delivery.

This problem is likely to have an impact on the following areas:

- The finance business process including efficiency, timeliness, clarity, accuracy, and relevancy
- The financial analysis and metrics business unit:
  - Definition (lack of financial vision, scope, and objectives)
  - Direction (misalignment with corporate vision)
  - Financial structure of the organization (currently no feasible method to measure the inefficient or inappropriateness of the current structure)
  - Financial performance (the product and service quality cannot be immediately measured in financial terms)
  - Financial data (validity and quality)
- Business location
  - Security of financial data (exposure and risks)
  - Relevancy of the current financial information
  - Finances (too expensive and these finances may not be able to be measured)

Business Opportunity

The following opportunities have been identified in this project:

- The availability and timeliness of key financial information

- The possibility that the business unit can respond rapidly to the changing environment by having up-to-the-minute information

- The ability to measure the cost and relevancy of the finance department and make further efficiencies

- The ability to support the transformation by adding financial information to operations

Requirements Statement

The requirements statement is a document that contains information about the needs and goals of an organization or project. This statement can be quite detailed, but often it is written at a summary level so as to be communicable to a broad range of people.

Business Drivers

The key business drivers for this project are as follows:

- An organizational transformation that must be achieved within two years

- A limited timeframe for competitive advantage

- Timing of other related changes to the business or external marketplace

Business Requirements

For each business problem (or opportunity) identified previously, document the detailed business requirements using the format shown in Figure 6-20.

Opportunities & Problems	Requirement
A lack of visibility of the key financials of the business and therefore no transparency.	Identify the key personal, the system, the data sources, and the technologies.
The availability and timeliness of key financial information.	Explore and evaluate all the current constraints and enablers and implement a process that will improve financial information efficiency by at least 50%.
The possibility that the business unit can respond rapidly to the changing environment by having up-to-the minute information.	Develop a tool that will enable the VP to analyze forecasts and predict future financial trends with 95% accuracy.
The ability to measure the cost and relevancy of the finance department and make further efficiencies.	Create a financial management suite (MIS) that will provide measurement metrics for all key financial drivers.
The ability to support the transformation by adding financial information to operations.	Develop a stable tool that will constantly achieve 99.9% availability.

Figure 6-20. A list of opportunities and problems is shown here

Feasibility Assessment

A number of assumptions need to be made as we cannot adequately take on a full feasibility assessment in this case study. So we should assume that we have now assessed and identified each of the solution's options available and the feasibility (or likelihood) of each option meeting the requirements defined in Figure 6-20.

In addition, we should assume that we have reviewed risks, issues, and assumptions associated with the feasibility of each option. The process for assessing the feasibility of an individual solution is shown in Figure 6-21.

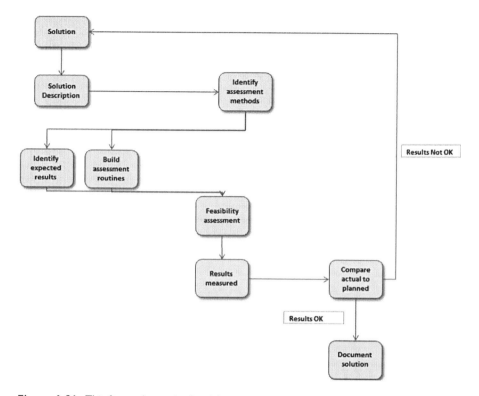

Figure 6-21. This figure shows the feasibility assessment process

Option One: Implementing Off-the-Shelf Software

This section gives a summary of the description of the option, the assessment, and the result.

Description

The option is to purchase a renowned software package such as one of the following:

- Quantrix Modeler
- IBM Cognos
- Oracle Hyperion
- Statistical Analysis Suite (SAS)

All the software mentioned will integrate with relational databases and provide a front-end interface that can be tailored to produce custom metrics and financial analysis.

Assessment

Here are the methods that have been used to assess the feasibility of this solution:

- Prototyping: This involved the construction of a demo software (called a prototype) to prove that at least a part of the full solution is achievable. In our example, the prototype was tested so that we could prove that the highest risk areas of the solution are feasible and to test that the package can be integrated into other application systems used for the business.

- Staff survey: This survey involved presenting the finance staff with a series of questions that had optional answers to assess their readiness and also their acceptance toward learning and using a new system.

Results

The expected result from the assessment for this solution is that there would not be any significant issues in the implementation. The actual results that were born from the prototyping support that assumption.

However, from the results from the staff survey, there would be a considerable cultural shift that would be required in order to use the software effectively.

Risks

There are some risks associated in the software implementation solution. These risks are defined as any event that may adversely affect the ability of the solution to produce the required deliverables. Risks may be strategic, environmental, financial, operational, technical, industrial, competitive, or customer-related. A list of the likely risks for our example is shown in Figure 6-22.

Description	Likelihood	Impact	Mitigating Actions
Inability to fully implement the software into Nonsuch systems.	Low	Very High	Outsource project to a company with proven industry experience and appropriately skilled implementation staff.
Technology solution is unable to deliver required results.	Medium	High	Complete a pilot project to prove the full technology solution.
Additional capital expenditure may be required in addition to that approved.	Medium	Medium	Maintain strict capital expenditure processes during the project.
Scope creep.	High	Medium	Get scope document approved and put in place change control process.
Additional training and cost for staff.	High	Medium	Make sure software vendor can assist with on-going training suited toward Nonsuch Corp.

Figure 6-22. A list of likely risks is shown here

When identifying the risks, I recommend that a formal risk assessment be undertaken and documented in a risk management plan to improve the likelihood and impact of each risk eventuating. Furthermore, a clear risk-management process (including risk forms and registers) should be used from the outset.

Issues

A list of current issues that adversely affect the ability of the solution to produce the required deliverables is included with Figure 6-23.

Description	Priority	Resolution Actions
Required capital expenditure funds have not been budgeted.	High	Request funding approval as part of this proposal.
Some of the required software is only at 'beta' phase and has not yet been released live.	Medium	Design a solution based on current software version and adapt changes to the solution once the final version of the software has been released.
There is a question as to the state of the data in the database.	High	A data audit and subsequent validation must ensue immediately.

Figure 6-23. A list of issues is shown here

Assumptions

This is a list of the assumptions associated with the adoption of this solution:

- There will be no legislative, business strategy, or policy changes during this project.

- Additional human resources will be available from the business to support the project.

- The organization as a whole will support the project.

Option Two: Developing a Financial Model Tool

This section gives a summary of the description of the option, the assessment, and the result.

Description

This option is to develop a dedicated financial model tool from a recognized financial modeling firm.

The model will be expected to integrate with existing relational databases and provide a front end that encapsulates all the outputs based upon the user requirements.

Assessment

Here are the methods that have been used to assess the feasibility of this solution:

- Prototyping: This involved the construction of a prototype financial model to test the validity of implementing the current databases and also running with the incumbent ERP system. In our example, the prototype was tested so that we could prove that the highest risk areas of the solution are feasible and to test that the package can be integrated into other application systems used for the business.

- Staff Survey: The survey involved presenting the finance staff with a series of question that had optional answers to assess their readiness and also their acceptance toward learning and using a new system.

Results

The expected result for this solution would be that there would not be any issues to implementing a financial modeling tool. The actual results born from the prototyping support this assumption.

The staff survey showed that while there would need to be a cultural shift, the negative effects of this shift could be minimized by making sure the staff members were involved throughout the development of the financial model tool.

Risks

There are some risks associated with the financial modeling tool solution. These risks are defined as any event that may adversely affect the ability of the solution to produce the required deliverables. Risks may be strategic, environmental, financial, operational, technical, industrial, competitive, or customer related. A list of the likely risks for our example is shown in Figure 6-24.

Description	Likelihood	Impact	Mitigating Actions
Inability to fully implement the modeling tool	Low	Very High	The financial modeling firm and modeler should be vetted and past results, successes, and failures considered.
Technology solution is unable to deliver required results	Medium	High	Complete a pilot project to prove the full technology solution.
Additional capital expenditure may be required in addition to that approved	Low	Medium	Maintain strict capital expenditure processes during the project.
Scope creep	High	Medium	A well-structured change control and a well-communicated scope will help to mitigate.
Additional training and cost for staff	Medium	Medium	Make sure the modeling firm can assist with ongoing training suited toward Nonsuch Corp.

Figure 6-24. This is a list of risks for Option Two

When identifying the risks, I recommend that a formal risk assessment be undertaken and documented in a risk-management plan to improve the likelihood and impact of each risk eventuating. Furthermore, a clear risk management process (including risk forms and registers) should be used from the outset.

Issues

A list of current issues that adversely affect the ability of the solution to produce the required deliverables is included with Figure 6-25.

Description	Priority	Resolution Actions
Required capital expenditure funds have not been budgeted.	High	Request funding approval as part of this proposal.
There is a question as to the state of the data in the database.	High	A data audit and subsequent validation must ensue immediately.

Figure 6-25. A list of issues for Option Two is shown here

Assumptions

This is a list the assumptions associated with the adoption of this solution:

- There will be no legislative, business strategy, or policy changes during this project.
- Additional human resources will be available from the business to support the project.
- The organization as a whole will support the project.

Feasibility Ranking

The ranking is a part of the feasibility assessment that compares the options, and then creates criteria and scores these against each option.

Ranking Criteria

The ranking criteria are provided in Figure 6-26.

Criteria	Option 1 Score	Option 1 Weight	Option 1 Total	Option 2 Score	Option 2 Weight	Option 2 Total
Cost	7	1.0	7.0	6	1.0	6.0
Benefit	9	1.5	13.5	9	1.5	13.5
Development/Implementation overrun	6	1.3	7.8	4	1.3	5.2
Business disruption	5	1.0	5	3	1.0	3
Flexibility to change specification	2	1.0	2	8	1.0	8
Cost of maintenance	7	0.7	4.9	5	0.7	3.5
Relative ease of staff adoption	6	1.4	8.4	8	1.4	11.2
Deliver precise outputs	6	1.5	9	9	1.5	13.5
Total Score	48.0		57.6	52.0		63.9

Figure 6-26. The criteria and ranking scores for both options are shown here

Ranking Scores

Score each option using the format shown in Figure 6-26.

■ **Note** The score is typically a number from 1 (low feasibility) to 10 (high feasibility), and the weight is a number from 0.5 (criterion is unimportant) to 1.5 (criterion is very important). The total is calculated as score x weight.

Feasibility Result

Option Two has achieved a higher total score and would therefore be the most feasible option for the solution. The key reason is down to its flexibility during the development. Therefore, the project can adapt to changes in the overall transformation program. Staff adaption would also be relatively easy because the staff would be actively involved in the development and implementation on an ongoing basis.

This chapter has covered several aspects of the model planning, and I would not expect anyone to understand all that has been mentioned in one reading. However, this chapter is one that must be understood because it's at the heart of the model design. Many of these concepts will also be featured again later in this book. If you have found any of the concepts unclear, I would advise that you read through this chapter again, focusing on a section at a time, and only move on once you have a clear understanding of that section.

CHAPTER

7

Financial-Based Calculations

If you recall from Chapter 2, one of the key modeling disciplines is the separation of inputs, calculations, and outputs. The outputs are linked to the calculations, and the calculations are linked to the inputs. Thus the calculations are in the middle—they are the link between the inputs and the outputs like the glue between two components.

I have purposely made sure that we only tackle the calculations once we have established both inputs and outputs because if you follow best practice, that is how the model develops. You want to start with outputs because they can be defined, follow up with the inputs because they originate from the drivers in the outputs, and afterward link the two elements with the calculations. Think of making a plastic model of an airplane. First, you need to understand what the final model should look like (the output). Then you subsequently check that all the parts to make the final model are available (the inputs). Finally, you piece it all together with the glue (the calculations), and so go financial models, hence why this chapter is the last of the three elements.

How to Lay Out Your Calculations

In my opinion, one of the worst sights in any model is where the calculations are badly laid out and resemble a jumble of functions and formula with no coherency. In other words, it's just plain ugly. In order to avoid establishing any bad habits with laying out calculations, I want to show you which formats will work best.

When I think of the layout of calculations, I am reminded of soldier ants, or worker ants. This will seem like a bizarre analogy, but you will soon understand the similarities. Ants always seem to have a purpose. There may be thousands of them in a colony, but if you watch them, you will notice that they are generally organized in a trail. They all follow the same unbroken and consistent path. Should something break that trail, they will scatter briefly. But in no time, they will establish the trail again and carry on with efficiency.

I want you to think of calculations in a similar vein. There are literally hundreds of formulas and functions, but they are all serving a single purpose: to link the inputs to the outputs. In doing so, it's more efficient if they follow an unbroken and consistent path, that no matter the complexity of the calculation, you can still recognize that it is a calculation and also where it is going.

In Figure 7-1, I have included a layout that I use in models. Notice first that once you are accustomed to the layout, it begins to look consistent. For example, all the narrative is down in a column, in this case column C. The calculations all begin from column E, and they are consistent across the row as can be seen in Figures 7-2 and 7-3.

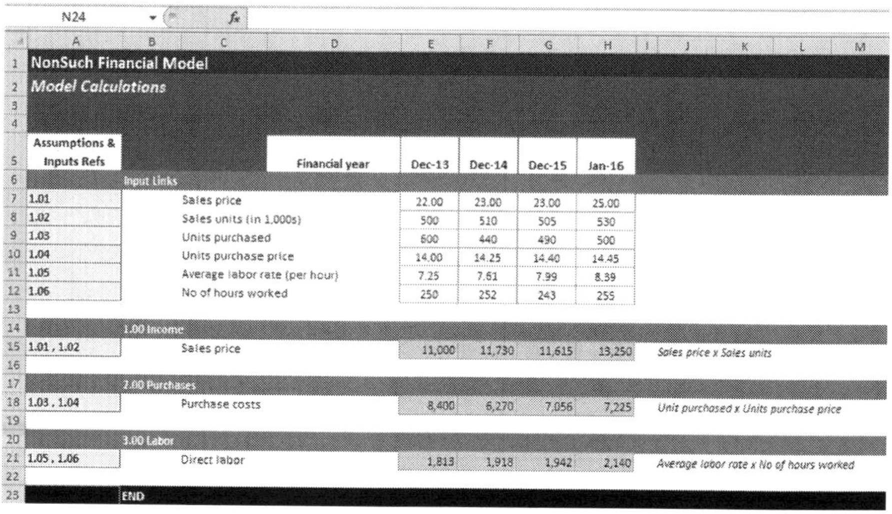

N24

NonSuch Financial Model

Model Calculations

Assumptions & Inputs Refs		Financial year	Dec-13	Dec-14	Dec-15	Jan-16	
	Input Links						
1.01	Sales price		22.00	23.00	23.00	25.00	
1.02	Sales units (in 1,000s)		500	510	505	530	
1.03	Units purchased		600	440	490	500	
1.04	Units purchase price		14.00	14.25	14.40	14.45	
1.05	Average labor rate (per hour)		7.25	7.61	7.99	8.39	
1.06	No of hours worked		250	252	243	255	
	1.00 Income						
1.01 , 1.02	Sales price		11,000	11,730	11,615	13,250	*Sales price x Sales units*
	2.00 Purchases						
1.03 , 1.04	Purchase costs		8,400	6,270	7,056	7,225	*Unit purchased x Units purchase price*
	3.00 Labor						
1.05 , 1.06	Direct labor		1,813	1,918	1,942	2,140	*Average labor rate x No of hours worked*
	END						

Figure 7-1. This figure shows a typical layout for the inputs

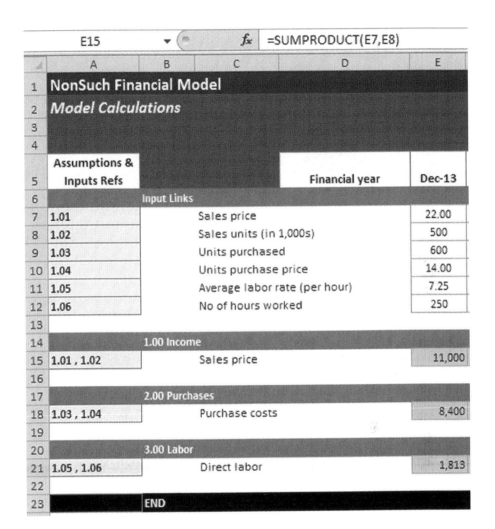

	E15		▼	f_x	=SUMPRODUCT(E7,E8)	
⊿	A	B	C	D	E
1	NonSuch Financial Model				
2	*Model Calculations*				
3					
4					
5	Assumptions & Inputs Refs			Financial year	Dec-13
6		Input Links			
7	1.01		Sales price		22.00
8	1.02		Sales units (in 1,000s)		500
9	1.03		Units purchased		600
10	1.04		Units purchase price		14.00
11	1.05		Average labor rate (per hour)		7.25
12	1.06		No of hours worked		250
13					
14		1.00 Income			
15	1.01 , 1.02		Sales price		11,000
16					
17		2.00 Purchases			
18	1.03 , 1.04		Purchase costs		8,400
19					
20		3.00 Labor			
21	1.05 , 1.06		Direct labor		1,813
22					
23		END			

Figure 7-2. Single SUMPRODUCT() function has been used Column E

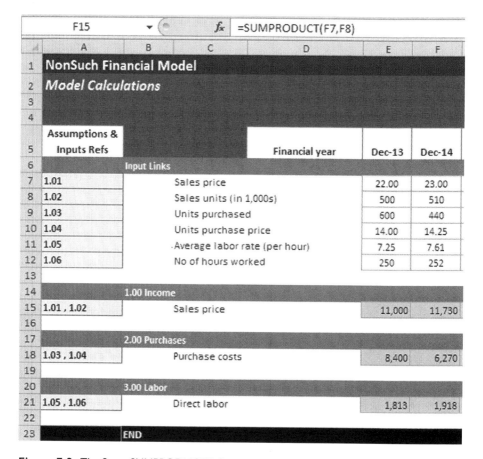

Figure 7-3. The Same SUMPRODUCT() function is used in column F as in Figure 7-2 to maintain consistency

In Figure 7-1, the inputs have been included in the calculation worksheet at the top of the worksheet just by creating a link. The reason for having these inputs for the calculation is to ensure that all the calculations are based on cells within the worksheet. You want to avoid having calculations that cross multiple worksheets because it will become very difficult to manage. It also becomes an excruciating problem when there are issues that need to be corrected in the model or when the model goes through testing or auditing.

Figure 7-4 is the input sheet, which provides the inputs to the calculation worksheet in Figure 7-5. Notice in this calculation worksheet that the links with the inputs have not been brought to the top of the worksheet, and so the formula references another worksheet. This contrasts the formula in Figure 7-2, which just references data within the worksheet.

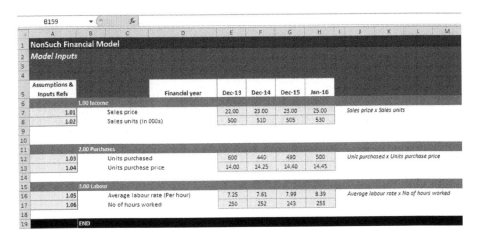

Figure 7-4. The input worksheet supports the calculations

	B159		fx									
	A	B	C	D	E	F	G	H	I	J	K	L	M
1	NonSuch Financial Model												
2	*Model Inputs*												
3													
4													
5	Assumptions & Inputs Refs			Financial year	Dec-13	Dec-14	Dec-15	Jan-16					
6		1.00 Income											
7	1.01		Sales price		22.00	23.00	23.00	25.00		Sales price x Sales units			
8	1.02		Sales units (in 000s)		500	510	505	530					
9													
10													
11		2.00 Purchases											
12	1.03		Units purchased		600	440	490	500		Unit purchased x Units purchase price			
13	1.04		Units purchase price		14.00	14.25	14.40	14.45					
14													
15		3.00 Labour											
16	1.05		Average labour rate (Per hour)		7.25	7.61	7.99	8.39		Average labour rate x No of hours worked			
17	1.06		No of hours worked		250	252	243	255					
18													
19		END											

	E10		fx	=SUMPRODUCT(Inputs!E12,Inputs!E13)								
	A	B	C	D	E	F	G	H	I	J	K	L	M
1	NonSuch Financial Model												
2	*Model Calculations*												
3													
4													
5	Assumptions & Inputs Refs			Financial year	Dec-13	Dec-14	Dec-15	Jan-16					
6		1.00 Income											
7	1.01 , 1.02		Sales price		11,000	11,730	11,615	13,250		Sales price x Sales units			
8													
9		2.00 Purchases											
10	1.03 , 1.04		Purchase costs		8,400	6,270	7,056	7,225		Unit purchased x Units purchase price			
11													
12		3.00 Labour											
13	1.05 , 1.06		Direct labour		1,813	1,918	1,942	2,140		Average labour rate x No of hours worked			
14													
15		END											

Figure 7-5. The calculations are drawing on the data in the input sheet as can be seen in the formula

These calculations may seem pedantic, but it's vital that you maintain consistency with the structure throughout the model when creating calculations. Make sure the inputs are brought into the calculation worksheet as links at the top and make all the calculations work from those links. This will make the model layout so much easier to navigate, and troubleshooting issues is then intuitive. Just be aware that often in a large and complicated model, there are a number of input worksheets. If you deviate from the practice of bringing input links into the calculations and make the formula go directly to the input sheet, you will have a function that references multiple worksheets. This will create a three-dimensional formula, like the one shown next, which makes the formula more intricate than it needs to be.

=SUMPRODUCT('Inputs 1'!E7:H7,'Inputs2'!E7:H7)

Not only is this formula messy and ugly, if you continue this way, you will at some point make a pointing error (referencing the incorrect cells by mistake). Once you have trawled through a few hundred functions to locate the error, it will become apparent why you should avoid this type of formula construction.

I have one last point to make about the layout for calculations. Going back to Figure 7-1, note that each calculation is a discrete calculation, that is, one item, one calculation. Although this seems obvious, don't be tempted to cut corners by make one almighty calculation that captures, for instance, sales income and purchase cost at once. The key here is to follow the input's layout as much as possible—so for every input, there should be a single calculation. It's fine to repeat the calculation again if necessary.

Using Best Practice Calculations

You may be wondering if I am about to give a list of functions that are considered best practice modeling. If this is your expectation, I have some bad news. There just isn't such a premise. Almost all of Excel's functions are ready for use by anyone, and they all have their own advantages and disadvantages. What makes them particularly effective is how they are applied and used. With that in mind, in this section, I will take you through a series of calculations (a situation that requires a calculation to be performed) and offer a solution of how to perform these calculations efficiently and follows best practice modeling.

Whole Range Calculations

The whole range calculation is an efficient calculation method with several benefits, particularly on large models. If you can invest some time setting up a range, I can assure it's well worth the effort. It involves giving a name to a series or a range of cells, and once that range has been named, it can then be used simply by referring to the name in the formula.

In Figures 7-6 and 7-7, take a look at the inputs at the top and the calculations below the inputs. At the top of the calculations, the input links have been brought into the calculations; however, instead of linking each cell across the eight years individually, I have referenced the name "Inp_Income" (input income). By using this name, I now only need to use the same name across the income row, and the link will give me the corresponding income amount. This method does away with having potential pointing areas because the modeler just needs to know the range name of each input row, which I have added in column L as a reference.

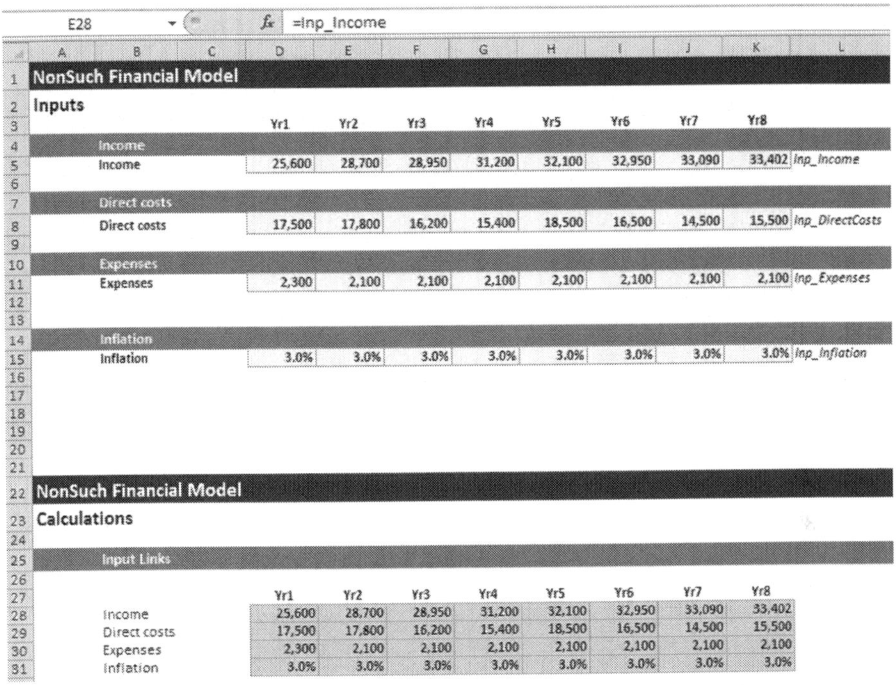

Figure 7-6. The cell in E28 has been linked to the range name Inp_Income

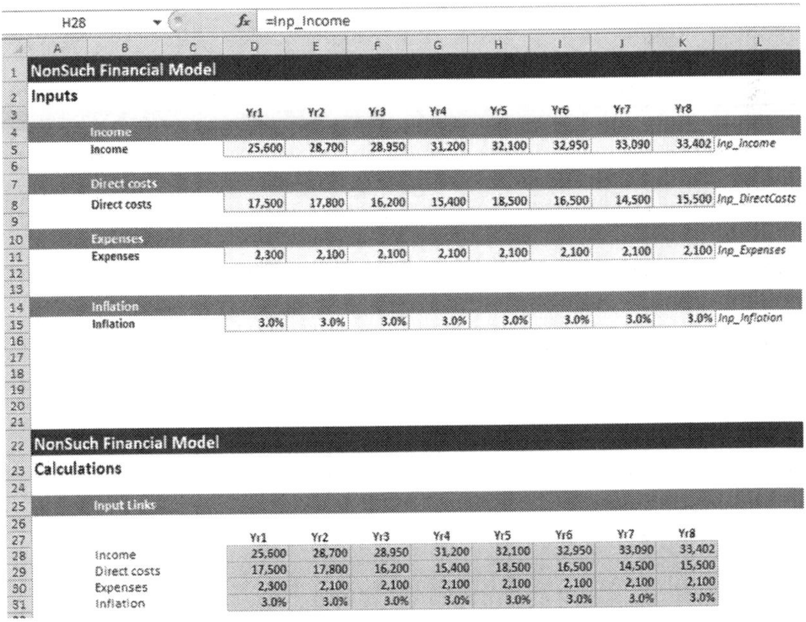

Figure 7-7. In this financial model, the whole range of cells from E28 to K28 references a single rage name called Inp_Income

Let's take a look now at how to create a whole range name:

Begin first by highlighting the whole range that will be named and make sure the starting column and the ending columns will remain consistent through the model. In Figure 7-8, columns D and K are the starting and ending columns, respectively.

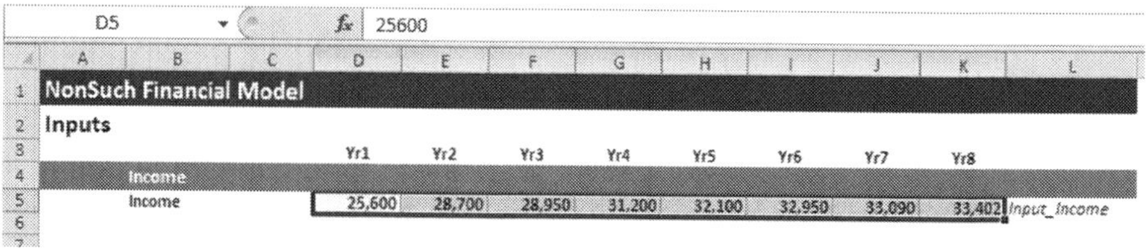

Figure 7-8. The first step is to highlight the full range that will be named

The range can then be named using the name box, which is located in the upper left of the worksheet just above the A and B column headings. Give the range an appropriate name (see Figure 7-9). By creating these range names, you can make calculations that are based on names. For example, to determine the gross income, you could write the following calculation:

$$Input\_Income *(1+Inputs\_SalesTax)$$

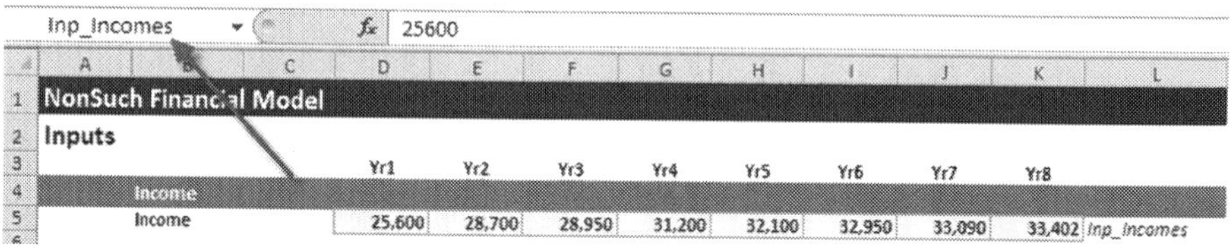

Figure 7-9. The whole range has been named "Inp_Income"

By using the whole range names, you can start to make calculations that when viewed become more meaningful. However, always make sure the columns are consistent, as any calculations that are made on inconsistent columns will mean that the results are unreliable (see Figure 7-10).

E18			f_x	=E15*(1+E16)						
A	B	C	D	E	F	G	H	I	J	K	L

1	NonSuch Financial Model										
2	Inputs										
3				Yr1	Yr2	Yr3	Yr4	Yr5	Yr6	Yr7	Yr8
4		Income									
5		Income		25,600	28,700	28,950	31,200	32,100	32,950	33,090	33,402 *Input_Income*
6											
7		Sales Tax									
8		Sales Tax		20.0%	20.0%	20.0%	20.0%	20.0%	20.0%	20.0%	20.0% *Input_SalesTax*
9											
10											
11											
12											
13	Calculations										
14		Actual Income									
15		Income			28,700	28,950	31,200	32,100	32,950	33,090	33,402	#VALUE!
16		Sales Tax			20.0%	20.0%	20.0%	20.0%	20.0%	20.0%	20.0%	#VALUE!
17											
18		Income with Sales Tax			34,440	34,740	37,440	38,520	39,540	39,708	40,082	#VALUE!

Figure 7-10. The columns between the inputs and calculations are misaligned, and therefore the calculations are unreliable

Calculating Time Periods

Making calculations that are based on time periods and time intervals can be very frustrating because of the conflict between what is pleasing and intuitive to the eye and what is practical and sensible modeling. To explain, see Figure 7-11. This is an all-too-typical situation. The modeler needs to produce some outputs, which are likely to be in a standard format based upon the client's requirements. The results do not look very appealing.

	A	B	C	D	E	F	G	H	I	J	K	L
1	NonSuch Financial Model											
2												
3	Outputs											
4												
5												
6			Quarter 1	Quarter 2	Quarter 3	Quarter 4	Year 1 Total	Quarter 1	Quarter 2	Quarter 3	Quarter 4	Year 2 Total
7		Income	5,800	5,950	5,004	5,101	21,855	5,740	5,703	5,649	5,830	22,922
8		Direct costs	2,700	2,710	3,920	2,700	12,030	2,750	2,755	2,790	2,700	10,995
9		Gross profit/(Loss)	3,100	3,240	1,084	2,700	10,124	2,990	2,948	2,859	3,130	11,927
10		Expenses	2,220	2,700	2,640	2,655	10,215	2,620	2,530	2,500	2,490	10,140
11		Net profit/(Loss)	880	540	(1,556)	45	(91)	370	418	359	640	1,787
12												
13	END											

Figure 7-11. The outputs are reported in quarters and years

In this model, the outputs are reporting in quarters and then totaled into years. Although there may appear to be nothing particularly harmful about such an output, it couldn't be further from the truth. This output is a disaster, and it really is the antithesis for any financial modeler. There is a lack of consistency across the columns as some are showing quarters and others are showing years; they should all the same timescale. In each row, there are four calculations for the quarters and then a different calculation on the total. One of the problems with this output is if you needed to reference it from another worksheet, you would be required to always check which cells are being used because some are in quarters and others are in years. The importance for modeling is to break this type into an output with quarters and an output with annual numbers in your calculations. By creating two separate calculations, you can then create outputs that give both quarterly and yearly numbers without breaking best practice consistency.

Different ways are available; one of the solutions is to use a tool called pivot tables. These pivot tables are very popular in financial circles, but there is just no room for them in financial modeling, such that I am not going to discuss them. In short, they are cumbersome and present major problems if you want to create calculation links from them. A better way is to use a calculation mask. A mask is a simple function that is created specifically to signal whether certain cells are included or excluded. Figure 7-12 is an example of a mask that has been created to accept time period quarters but nothing else.

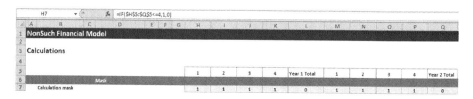

Figure 7-12. In this model, the calculation mask is being used on the time periods

You can see that the quarters are simply labeled 1, 2, 3, and 4. It's generally easier to perform calculations on labels if they are numbers and not text. I have named the table with the time periods "TableHeadings," which makes it simpler for referencing. The formula in the mask simply states that if a number is less than or equal to 4 (there are 4 quarters for a year), then return a number one. Otherwise, return a zero. This mask can now be used to include or exclude quarters and annual amounts as in Figure 7-13.

H18 =H10*Calc_Mask

NonSuch Financial Model

Calculations

	1	2	3	4	Year 1 Total	1	2	3	4	Year 2 Total
Mask										
Calculation mask	1	1	1	1	0	1	1	1	1	0
Net profit calculation										
Income	5,800	5,950	5,004	5,101	21,855	5,740	5,703	5,649	5,830	22,922
Direct costs	2,700	2,710	3,920	2,700	12,030	2,750	2,755	2,790	2,700	10,995
Gross profit/(Loss)	3,100	3,240	1,084	2,700	10,124	2,990	2,948	2,859	3,130	11,927
Expenses	2,220	2,700	2,640	2,655	10,215	2,620	2,530	2,500	2,490	10,140
Net profit/(Loss)	880	540	(1,556)	45	(91)	370	418	359	640	1,787
Net profit calculation (Quarters)										
Income	5,800	5,950	5,004	5,101	-	5,740	5,703	5,649	5,830	-
Direct costs	2,700	2,710	3,920	2,700	-	2,750	2,755	2,790	2,700	-
Gross profit/(Loss)	3,100	3,240	1,084	2,700	-	2,990	2,948	2,859	3,130	-
Expenses	2,220	2,700	2,640	2,655	-	2,620	2,530	2,500	2,490	-
Net profit/(Loss)	880	540	(1,556)	45	-	370	418	359	640	-

Figure 7-13. The calculation mask is used to include quarters but not years

The process is to multiply the quarterly numbers with the calculation mask, and anything that is multiplied by zero produces a zero. This way you can completely eradicate the annual amounts. The next part is to produce a table that just takes the yearly amounts and excludes the quarters; this step is slightly harder because you are now reversing the use of the zero and the one, as in Figure 7-14.

H25 =IF(Calc_Mask=1,0,SUMPRODUCT($H$7:H$7,$H10:H10))-C25

NonSuch Financial Model

Calculations

	1	2	3	4	Year 1 Total	1	2	3	4	Year 2 Total
Mask										
Calculation mask	1	1	1	1	0	1	1	1	1	0
Net profit calculation										
Income	5,800	5,950	5,004	5,101	21,855	5,740	5,703	5,649	5,830	22,922
Direct costs	2,700	2,710	3,920	2,700	12,030	2,750	2,755	2,790	2,700	10,995
Gross profit/(Loss)	3,100	3,240	1,084	2,700	10,124	2,990	2,948	2,859	3,130	11,927
Expenses	2,220	2,700	2,640	2,655	10,215	2,620	2,530	2,500	2,490	10,140
Net profit/(Loss)	880	540	(1,556)	45	(91)	370	418	359	640	1,787
Net profit calculation (Quarters)										
Income	5,800	5,950	5,004	5,101	-	5,740	5,703	5,649	5,830	-
Direct costs	2,700	2,710	3,920	2,700	-	2,750	2,755	2,790	2,700	-
Gross profit/(Loss)	3,100	3,240	1,084	2,700	-	2,990	2,948	2,859	3,130	-
Expenses	2,220	2,700	2,640	2,655	-	2,620	2,530	2,500	2,490	-
Net profit/(Loss)	880	540	(1,556)	45	-	370	418	359	640	-
Net profit calculation (Annual)										
Income	-	-	-	-	21,855	-	-	-	-	22,922
Direct costs	-	-	-	-	12,030	-	-	-	-	10,995
Gross profit/(Loss)	-	-	-	-	10,124	-	-	-	-	11,927
Expenses	-	-	-	-	10,215	-	-	-	-	10,140
Net profit/(Loss)	-	-	-	-	(91)	-	-	-	-	1,787

Figure 7-14. In this model, the calculation mask is used to include the years and exclude the quarters

The calculation now will exclude anything that has a one in the mask and will include anything with zero.

Calculating Depreciation

Calculating asset depreciation used to be a major problem because Excel didn't have a dedicated function to handle the different depreciation methods. I have included this calculation not because it is best practice, but because few modelers or Excel users realize that Microsoft actually included a few depreciation calculations in Excel 2007 (and later versions)—the SLN(), SYD(), DB() and DDB()—which have now simplified the entire depreciation calculation.

When I create depreciation calculations in financial models, I aim to make them clear and clean. I also make one set of calculations for every asset as in Figure 7-15. This is the only real hassle with depreciation calculations; I have seen models where the assets have been grouped in order to save time. Be very careful with grouping—much will depend upon the classification of the assets and the type of allowances that are allowed by the tax authorities. Simply grouping them together could get you into major trouble if you haven't taken authoritative tax advice. Therefore, it is better to make individual calculations that can be altered very quickly should any changes be required.

	A	B	C	D	E
1	NonSuch Financial Model				
2	Calculations				
3					
4		Input Links			
5		Asset:	Original Cost:	Life (Years):	Salvage Value:
6		Printer	$35,000	7	$500

Figure 7-15. The inputs for the depreciation calculation are referenced from the calculation worksheet

For all the depreciation methods, there are four requirements or details that will be required. Don't worry if you are unable to get these details from the inputs. The prominent part is that the calculations are set up correctly as in Figure 7-16. This way, the inputs can just be assumptions, and again this is where it is important that each asset be calculated separately to avoid mixing different asset life of each asset and depreciation rates. The asset life, which is the predicted number of years that an asset is expected to be useful, is very important because it will govern the rate at which that asset should be depreciated. In Figure 7-16, there is an expected seven-year asset life.

G30		f_x			
	A	B	C	D	E	F

NonSuch Financial Model

Calculations

Input Links

Asset:	Original Cost:	Life (years):	Salvage Value:
Printer	$35,000	7	$500

Depreciation Calculation

Depreciation Amount

Year	SLN	DB	DDB	SYD
1	$4,928.57	$15,925.00	$10,000.00	$8,625.00
2	$4,928.57	$8,679.13	$7,142.86	$7,392.86
3	$4,928.57	$4,730.12	$5,102.04	$6,160.71
4	$4,928.57	$2,577.92	$3,644.31	$4,928.57
5	$4,928.57	$1,404.96	$2,603.08	$3,696.43
6	$4,928.57	$765.71	$1,859.34	$2,464.29
7	$4,928.57	$417.31	$1,328.10	$1,232.14

Figure 7-16. This model displays the depreciation calculations

The calculations are then relatively straightforward. I find it simpler to create a calculation table of the number in columns rather than rows because it is much easier to create a lookup from a column in a table if needed. There are four widely practiced depreciation methods:

- Straight-line method
- Declining balance method
- Double-declining balance method
- Sum of the year's digits method

I will not be describing depreciation strategies or methods in this book, as it is an extensive topic. If you want to gain a solid understanding of depreciation, the best way is to find a tax accountant who is willing to explain it to you. Firsthand knowledge when discussing depreciation is invaluable. The other alternative would be to purchase a good accounting book.

However, for this book, based upon my experience the majority of modeling projects will use the straight-line method. If you create a table like in Figure 7-16, you will have all the methods calculated. Notice in Figure 7-16 how each of the methods produces different depreciation rates, which is why it is important that the method used can be justified accordingly. Here are the functions that represent the methods:

- =SLN() Straight-line method
- =DB() Declining balance method
- =DDB() Double-declining balance method
- =SYD() Sum of the years digits' method

Each of these functions uses the mix of the four inputs elements. For instance, the straight-line method requires the original cost, asset life, and salvage value, while the declining balance also requires the year, as in Figure 7-17.

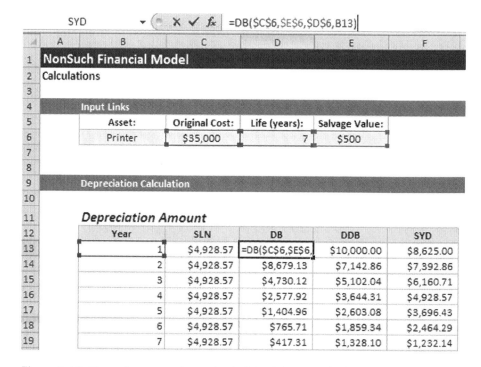

Figure 7-17. These elements make up the declining balance method

In addition to creating a deprecation calculation, you should also create a table that shows the value of the asset in each year after it has been depreciated, as in Figure 7-18. This information will be needed for the balance sheet in the fixed assets. The formula is calculated by taking the starting value of the asset and taking off the depreciation amount based upon the depreciation calculation each year. Then use the balance again to deduct the depreciation the following year.

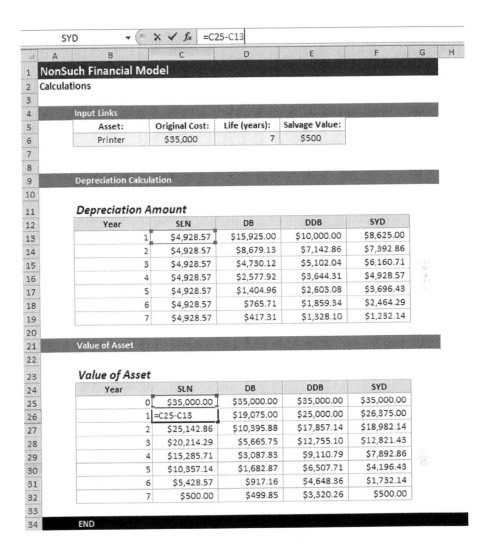

Figure 7-18. This model shows the value of the assets after depreciation

Database Calculations

At some point, it is very likely that the modeler will need to work with data tables. Data tables are sets of data, which consist of headings and several rows of data under these headings like in Figure 7-19.

7	**NonSuch Financial Model**			
8	Inputs (Data)			
9				

	Month	Employee	Region	Age	Annual Earnings
10					
11	Jan	Susan	Northern	42	283,800
12	Jan	Chris	Western	40	507,200
13	Jan	Jamie	Eastern	38	107,600
14	Jan	Randy	Southern	46	391,600
15	Jan	Anil	Northern	36	226,700
16	Feb	Yasmin	Northern	48	411,800
17	Feb	Vladimir	Northern	29	154,200
18	Feb	Jason	Southern	33	258,000
19	Feb	Coreen	Southern	34	233,800

Figure 7-19. A data table is a set of data consisting of headings and rows of data

These databases are formed when the modeler has to collect and collate much information from various sources, which then need to be grouped. They are also needed when importing information such as when a comma-separated values (CSV) file from an external data source is required. Fortunately, there are a number of functions in Excel that can ease the burden of calculation from large data tables, and they are collectively known as the database function. There are twelve database functions that can be identified by the "D" on the start of the function name, such as DSUM(), which provide help with counting the data, determining totals, or getting the average.

I am often surprised at how seldom modelers use these functions when in fact they are quite simple to use and, when used effectively, are powerful and not processor-intensive. Every financial modeler should be comfortable with knowing when and how to use these database functions.

To demonstrate, look again at Figure 7-19, which is a database that consists of names with their locations, age, and annual earnings. Typically, these would be the data inputs in the model, and normally a number of calculations would be created with this data. When dealing with data like this in a table, the modeler should assume that the user of the model is going to want to see the effects on the model outputs based on different views of the data. For instance, the user may want to see the total of all salaries in the northern regions or the total high test salary in the southern region. The use of data tables allows for greater flexibility, because any changes in the content of the model is applied by changing the data in the table and not the structure of the model.

All the database functions have similar requirements—they all need to have a table of data, a column that will be referenced, and a criterion. In Figure 7-20a, I have provided a criterion that consists of a cut-down version of the table in Figure 7-19. The column headings will be used as the criteria. In the example, the criteria is for the month of Jan (January), but you could just as easily select a region and an age as well that would then make the criteria multifaceted. Note that there is only one row of criteria available; however, this is only because I have chosen to construct the inputs that way. In fact, I could just as easily add a second or third row to the criteria, as in Figure 7-20b.

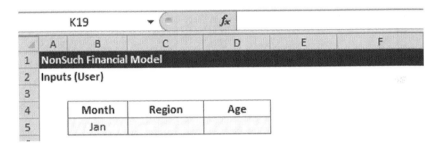

Figure 7-20a. This figure shows the inputs criteria

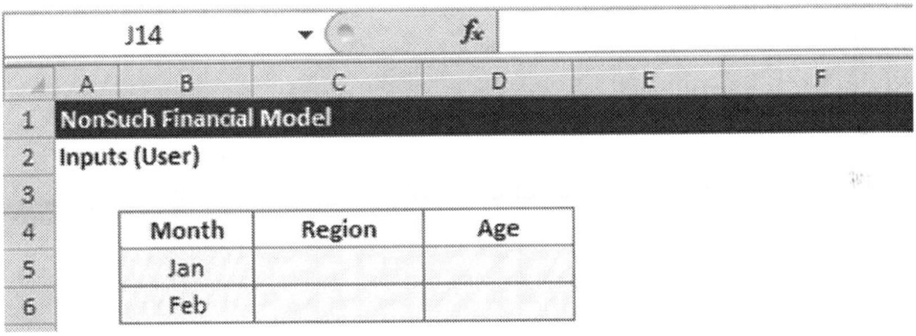

Figure 7-20b. This figure shows a multi-row criteria input

When dealing with large data sets, it is useful to be able to provide a criteria selection that can handle more than one parameter for each heading, However, for our example, we only need the one row as in Figure 7-20a.

In Figure 7-21a, the inputs from the criteria have been brought into the inputs links. Four database calculations have now been created by using four functions: DSUM, DAVERAGE, DMAX, and DMIN. The syntax for each of these functions is as follows:

=DFUNCTIONNAME(Full table, Reference column, Full criteria).

23	NonSuch Financial Model	
24	Calculations	
25		
26	Input Links	
27		
28	Month	Jan
29	Region	0
30	Age	0
31	Database Calculations	
32		
33	Total for input selection	1,516,900
34	Average for input selection	303,380
35	Maximum for input selection	507,200
36	Minimum for input selection	107,600

Figure 7-21a. This figure shows the database functions' calculations

In Figure 7-21b, the formula for the DSUM can show that it is accessing the table in the range B11:F20, the reference column is the annual earning in column F row 11, and the criteria are the inputs in B4:D5.

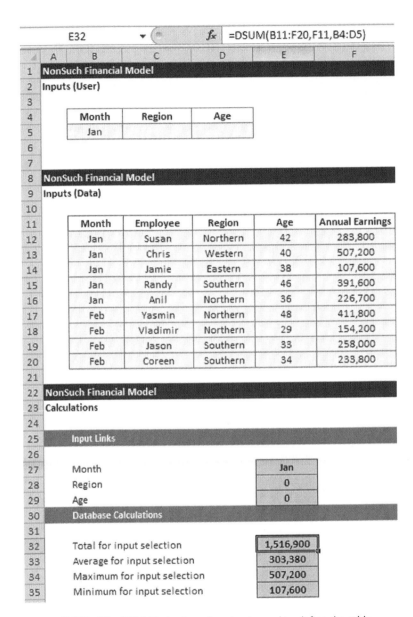

| E32 | ▼ | | *fx* | =DSUM(B11:F20,F11,B4:D5) |

	A	B	C	D	E	F
1	NonSuch Financial Model					
2	Inputs (User)					
3						
4		Month	Region	Age		
5		Jan				
6						
7						
8	NonSuch Financial Model					
9	Inputs (Data)					
10						
11		Month	Employee	Region	Age	Annual Earnings
12		Jan	Susan	Northern	42	283,800
13		Jan	Chris	Western	40	507,200
14		Jan	Jamie	Eastern	38	107,600
15		Jan	Randy	Southern	46	391,600
16		Jan	Anil	Northern	36	226,700
17		Feb	Yasmin	Northern	48	411,800
18		Feb	Vladimir	Northern	29	154,200
19		Feb	Jason	Southern	33	258,000
20		Feb	Coreen	Southern	34	233,800
21						
22	NonSuch Financial Model					
23	Calculations					
24						
25		Input Links				
26						
27		Month			Jan	
28		Region			0	
29		Age			0	
30		Database Calculations				
31						
32		Total for input selection			1,516,900	
33		Average for input selection			303,380	
34		Maximum for input selection			507,200	
35		Minimum for input selection			107,600	

Figure 7-21b. The DSUM() database function is used to define the table

The database calculations have a number of uses because they are reliant on the criteria. They are also very versatile and can be used to engage the model user to create "what if?" scenarios. Another use for the calculations is to provide dashboard information for the model. I often use the database functions to provide feedback to the model user about the status of the data based upon the user selection (see Figure 7-22).

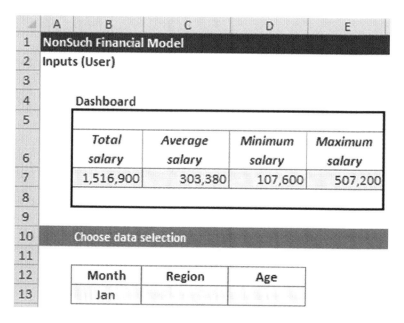

Figure 7-22. The database calculations are used in a dashboard

Another use for the functions is for internal admin for the model. These functions can be used to check for changes in the model that have occurred after the model has been opened and to report on those changes. This information can then be placed in a user log with a date and timestamp, which provides admin information of when changes to the model were made.

Calculating Net Present Value (NPV)

The net present value (NPV) is one of those calculations that is a must for modelers. Whether it is being used on the model that you have built or not, every modeler should be able to calculate the NPV and be aware of the short-comings of using the NPV function in Excel.

In Figure 7-23, I have used four time periods, 0 to 3. These can be months or years, but with this example they will be called time periods. The NPV function has the following syntax:

=NPV(Discount NPV (Discount rate, cash flows), rate, cash flows).

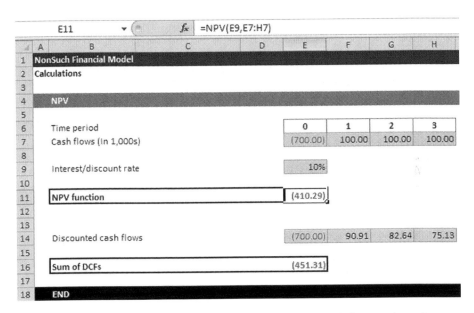

E11		f_x =NPV(E9,E7:H7)				

	A	B	C	D	E	F	G	H
1	NonSuch Financial Model							
2	Calculations							
3								
4	NPV							
5								
6		Time period				0	1	2	3
7		Cash flows (In 1,000s)				(700.00)	100.00	100.00	100.00
8								
9		Interest/discount rate				10%			
10								
11		NPV function				(410.29)			
12								
13								
14		Discounted cash flows				(700.00)	90.91	82.64	75.13
15								
16		Sum of DCFs				(451.31)			
17								
18	END							

Figure 7-23. The NPV calculation of the sum of the discounted cash flows is shown here

In the example, the discount rate is 10%, and the cash flows are in row 7.

In addition to the NPV, there is also a calculation for the discounted cash flows in row 14, which uses the cash flows, discount rate, and time periods. I have provided the sum of the discounted cash flows (DCFs) to give a check on the NPV.

The sum of the discounted cash flows should always equal the NPV value, but as can be seen in Figure 7-23, that is not the case. This means there must be an issue with either how the function has been used or the calculation itself. Fortunately, I am aware that the Excel NPV calculation is flawed because it doesn't actually give the NPV. What it does give is a present value (PV), and unless an adjustment is made the NPV will be incorrect.

To understand the flaw in the NPV function, think about what happens when a project starts. You can assume that the investment for the project is made up front, and so you would call this time period "zero" (Day 0). The cash flows for the project will start to flow from the time period 1 onwards, but as the investment is made on time period 0, it should not be included in the discounted cash flows.

Unfortunately, the Excel NPV function has a built-in assumption that even the first cash flow, which is the investment, happens at the end of the year. Although in reality, the initial investment is almost always made up front as there are likely to be up-front costs, such as deposits and capital that must be secured prior to the project commencing. With this understanding, you would need to adjust the NPV calculation to reflect this reality, which means adding the investment without discounting and then using the NPV function to discount the rest of the cash flows.

A further issue with the NPV function is that it assumes that the cash flows are at the end of time period. So, for instance, if the time periods are annual (years), it assumes that the cash received for the investment is in the very last month, and is therefore not realistic. The modeler should be aware of this feature of the function and be prepared to explain this to model users.

In Figure 7-24, the correct version of the NPV function has been used. The cash flow has been shortened to reflect period 1 to period 3 as the cash flows to be discounted by using the discount rate 10%. The initial investment has subsequently been added back undiscounted. To see of the calculation is correct, it can be checked by testing it against the total of the discounted cash flows in Figure 7-24 to make sure the NPV and the DCFs are the same, which now works.

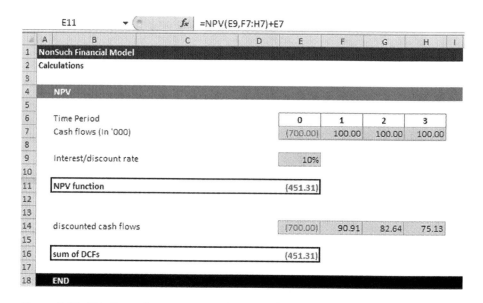

Figure 7-24. This figure shows a corrected version of the NPV function

It is imperative that modelers have a solid understanding of how to make the NPV calculation correctly. This understanding will ensure that mistakes are not made during the NPV calculation. This is a key financial calculation, so be sure you really understand how to make NPV calculations correctly.

Indices Calculations

A very frequent calculation, particularly in models where there is historical data or forecast data, is creating indices. Indices are useful because they give a view of trends quickly and also provide a method of comparing two or more items against each other. They also make very good visual representations for graphs. While they are simple to create, it is surprising how often I have seen indices created incorrectly inside models. The basic tenet of the calculation is to create a growth data based on this calculation:

(The period that is being measured minus the previous period) divided by the period being measured.

The result from the growth data should be applied to the base year (the year that will be used to measure differences in growth):

Base Year times (1 plus Growth Data)

Figure 7-25a features data about the price of a Big Mac converted into US dollars across a series of nations (taken from the Big Mac Index published by *The Economist*).

	J22			f_x
	A	B	C	D
1				
2	The Price of a Big Mac (In US$)			
3		2008	2009	2010
4	Australia	3.36	3.37	3.84
5	Brazil	4.73	4.02	4.91
6	Britain	4.57	3.69	3.48
7	Canada	4.08	3.35	4.00
8	China	1.83	1.83	1.95
9	Hong Kong	1.71	1.72	1.90
10	Norway	7.88	6.15	7.20
11	Russia	2.54	2.04	2.33
12	South Africa	2.24	2.17	2.45
13	United States	3.57	3.57	3.73

Figure 7-25a. The table shows the price of a Big Mac in US dollars across different nations

You need to apply the calculation to each of these time periods, as in Figure 7-25b.

C17			f_x =(C4-B4)/C4	
	A	B	C	D	E
1					
2	The Price of a Big Mac (In US$)				
3		2008	2009	2010	
4	Australia	3.36	3.37	3.84	
5	Brazil	4.73	4.02	4.91	
6	Britain	4.57	3.69	3.48	
7	Canada	4.08	3.35	4.00	
8	China	1.83	1.83	1.95	
9	Hong Kong	1.71	1.72	1.90	
10	Norway	7.88	6.15	7.20	
11	Russia	2.54	2.04	2.33	
12	South Africa	2.24	2.17	2.45	
13	United States	3.57	3.57	3.73	
14					
15	Growth Data				
16		2008	2009	2010	
17	Australia		0.3%	12.2%	
18	Brazil		(17.7%)	18.1%	
19	Britain		(23.8%)	(6.0%)	

Figure 7-25b. The growth data is calculated by comparing the change from the previous year

Note the calculation in Figure 7-25b. This is the root of the index calculation. While it is simple, just be careful to use the parentheses in the right place. You should be aware that indices can also be shown as proportion of 100, as in Figure 7-25c.

C30			f_x	=B30*(1+C17)
A	B	C	D	E

	A	B	C	D	E
1					
2	The Price of a Big Mac (In US$)				
3		2008	2009	2010	
4	Australia	3.36	3.37	3.84	
5	Brazil	4.73	4.02	4.91	
6	Britain	4.57	3.69	3.48	
7	Canada	4.08	3.35	4.00	
8	China	1.83	1.83	1.95	
9	Hong Kong	1.71	1.72	1.90	
10	Norway	7.88	6.15	7.20	
11	Russia	2.54	2.04	2.33	
12	South Africa	2.24	2.17	2.45	
13	United States	3.57	3.57	3.73	
14					
15	Growth Data				
16		2008	2009	2010	
17	Australia		0.3%	12.2%	
18	Brazil		(17.7%)	18.1%	
19	Britain		(23.8%)	(6.0%)	
20	Canada		(21.8%)	16.3%	
21	China		-	6.2%	
22	Hong Kong		0.6%	9.5%	
23	Norway		(28.1%)	14.6%	
24	Russia		(24.5%)	12.4%	
25	South Africa		(3.2%)	11.4%	
26	United States		-	4.3%	
27					
28	Index Data				
29		2008	2009	2010	
30	Australia	100	100.30	112.57	
31	Brazil	100	82.34	97.26	
32	Britain	100	76.15	71.56	

Figure 7-25c. The growth data is applied to the base year to give an index

The index is now created and can be used to reflect changes in growth against the base year as in Figure 7-25d.

D41			f_x
A	B	C	D
2 The Price of a Big Mac (In US$)			
3	2008	2009	2010
4 Australia	3.36	3.37	3.84
5 Brazil	4.73	4.02	4.91
6 Britain	4.57	3.69	3.48
7 Canada	4.08	3.35	4.00
8 China	1.83	1.83	1.95
9 Hong Kong	1.71	1.72	1.90
10 Norway	7.88	6.15	7.20
11 Russia	2.54	2.04	2.33
12 South Africa	2.24	2.17	2.45
13 United States	3.57	3.57	3.73
14			
15 Growth Data			
16	2008	2009	2010
17 Australia		0.3%	12.2%
18 Brazil		(17.7%)	18.1%
19 Britain		(23.8%)	(6.0%)
20 Canada		(21.8%)	16.3%
21 China		-	6.2%
22 Hong Kong		0.6%	9.5%
23 Norway		(28.1%)	14.6%
24 Russia		(24.5%)	12.4%
25 South Africa		(3.2%)	11.4%
26 United States		-	4.3%
27			
28 Index Data			
29	2008	2009	2010
30 Australia	100	100.30	112.57
31 Brazil	100	82.34	97.26
32 Britain	100	76.15	71.56
33 Canada	100	78.21	90.92
34 China	100	100.00	106.15
35 Hong Kong	100	100.58	110.11
36 Norway	100	71.87	82.35
37 Russia	100	75.49	84.89
38 South Africa	100	96.77	107.83
39 United States	100	100.00	104.29

Figure 7-25d. This is a layout for the full index table, which would be placed in the outputs of the model

This chapter has discussed the difficult concept of financial-based calculations. They are difficult because there can be several different methods of performing the calculations, and each has its own foibles. A big fear for modelers is making mistakes when performing calculations in models. Unfortunately, I cannot tell that you won't make mistakes. However, even if you do make mistakes, understanding how and why those mistakes were made is the key better modeling.

Logical-and Structural-Based Calculations

In this chapter, I want to take a look at functions that fit into a specific part of modeling. I will be discussing functions that work with dates, lookup functions, mathematical functions, and also some functions that are specific to particular situations. I will also outline the functions that fit into various modeling structures and point out functions that modelers should be learning to use. In financial modeling, there are no defined methods of using functions; in fact, there are no prescribed functions for any given modeling situation. The functions that are used in models are instead a reflection of the modeler's skills, experience, and understanding of best practice modeling.

Array Calculations for Single Values

In this section, I want to show you how to use array functions to solve calculation problems. Array calculations have their uses in modeling because they allow the modeler to create calculations that are tailored toward the results that are required. An array formula is a formula that works with an array, or series, of data values rather than an individual data value. There are two types of array formulas. The first type returns a singular value to a single cell and works with a series of data and aggregates it, typically using SUM, AVERAGE, or COUNT. The second type returns an array of values as their result into two or more cells. This section will demonstrate the use of a number of array calculations that are very practical for modeling and, in doing so, will offer the premise for using the array formula while still maintaining a best-practice model.

The first example is how to force a calculation on a series of data even when there is an error. Keep in mind that Excel is a very logical application. If it encounters an error for a series of data, then it's impossible to make any calculations on the data series without picking that error. In other words, it won't calculate just using traditional functions (see Figure 8-1).

	D12		▼	f_x {=AVERAGE(IF(ISERROR(D4:D10),"",D4:D10))}		
◢	A	B	C	D	E	
1						
2						
3		Purchased Units	Unit Cost	Average Cost per Unit		
4		200	20.00	20.00		
5		350	35.00	27.50		
6		280	twenty	#VALUE!		
7		230	23.00	#VALUE!		
8		60	6.00	14.50		
9		390	39.00	22.50		
10		340	34.00	36.50		
11						
12		Average Cost of Units (Ignore Errors)		24.200		

Figure 8-1. This model is using the average function as an array to calculate over errors

In the calculation, the formula is calculating an average cost per unit. But I have added in an extra dimension so that if an error occurs in the column where I am reading data (column D), then I can just substitute the error with blank data (" ") and calculate the average. Otherwise, calculate the average as usual. (The syntax of the formula is not explained for the reason that it will be explained in the next section.)

This array function is extremely useful because it can be used to check the inputs, and even if the inputs are in error, the calculation is still made. However, always be aware that when using such a calculation with averages, the result will be skewed because there is some missing data. Notice the curly braces around the formula. Do not be tempted to place these braces yourself as they are automatically created when you type Ctrl, Shift, and Enter, which is how to create arrays.

Formulas That Are Based on Condition

This next array calculation is based on creating a formula that will give results based upon a condition. Again, this is another classic example of a situation that comes up repeatedly in financial models. The SUMIF function, while extremely useful, is not capable of handling conditions beyond two dimensions without having to make a highly complex formula. I know of several modelers who are very uncomfortable with using arrays, but there is nothing to fear. Yes, it's not good practice to have hundreds of arrays strewn through the model. But at the same time, you should be capable of using them when required to do so. In Figure 8-2, I have created a simple conditional calculation that illustrates the use of COUNT, but this can be expanded to take on several more conditions or used with SUM, AVERAGE, or even SUMPRODUCT.

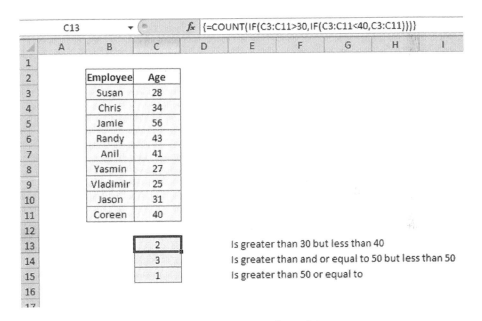

Figure 8-2. This model uses the array calculation with conditions

Notice the syntax. The IF statement in Figure 8-2 is looking for two conditions in the table. The first condition is finding where the age is greater than 30, and the second condition is to find where the age is less than 40. The return is to show how many occurrences happen with these conditions. There is an IF placed for each condition. It is possible to have several more conditions (up to seven), but I would argue that anything beyond three conditions is excessive. At that stage, you would start to verge on using online analytical processing (OLAP) cubes, which will not be covered in this book.

OLAP cubes would be used on tables of data and information where one row of data can have several columns of information because the formula is able to accommodate several conditions.

Getting the Closest Match to an Input Target

This next array calculation is one that I have used in order to test the data for a specific target. Put simply, the formula allows the user to input a target, which can be text or a numeric value depending on which part of the data the calculation is referencing. By then entering the target inputs, the formula checks through the data range and picks out the item that comes closest to matching the target.

This array formula is very useful for checking the tolerance in a date, for instance. When I create models that are required to receive a download of a CSV file from an external data store of personal data, I will often have this target input in place. This way, I can check to see any of the ages, for example in Figure 8-3, are near zero or 100, as that will provide me with highest and lowest tolerances. If the closest match falls below or above this range, then I can be reasonably sure that the data is lacking integrity.

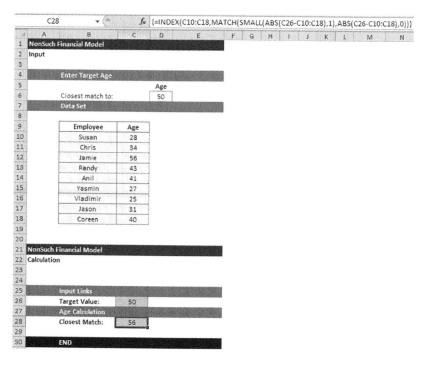

Figure 8-3. The input is used to set the target age, and the closest match is identified

Using Crosstab Calculations

For those who have used relational databases such as Microsoft Access, you should already be aware of the crosstab. This is a method of summarizing categorical data by using an algorithm that searches between those categories. Crosstab calculations are far from essential to modeling, but they are useful, particularly for representing data in a logical manner. I use crosstab calculations mainly for presenting dashboards by creating tables that can easily be digested. Figure 8-4 shows how a cross table can be created with an array calculation.

	C24		f_x {=SUM(($B24=$B$4:$B$20)*(C$23=$C$4:$C$20)*$D$4:$D$20)}						

	A	B	C	D	E	F	G	H	I
1									
2									
3		Date	Category	Amount					
4		11/08/2014	Expense	23,500					
5		11/08/2014	Expense	15,000					
6		11/08/2014	Expense	9,120					
7		11/08/2014	Revenue	16,950					
8		11/08/2014	Direct cost	145,500					
9		16/02/2014	Revenue	65,950					
10		16/02/2014	Revenue	20,000					
11		16/02/2014	Revenue	7,800					
12		03/03/2014	Revenue	20,000					
13		03/03/2014	Direct cost	89,000					
14		03/03/2014	Direct cost	9,000					
15		03/03/2014	Direct cost	3,500					
16		06/01/2014	Direct cost	11,020					
17		06/01/2014	Direct cost	78,440					
18		06/01/2014	Direct cost	75,300					
19		23/12/2014	Taxation	11,500					
20		23/12/2014	Expense	15,500					
21									
22									
23			Expense	Revenue	Direct cost	Lodging	Taxation		
24		11-Aug	47,620	16,950	145,500	-	-		
25		16-Feb	-	93,750	-	-	-		
26		06-Jan	-	-	164,760	-	-		
27		03-Mar	-	20,000	101,500	-	-		
28		23-Dec	15,500	-	-	-	11,500		

Figure 8-4. A crosstab calculation is useful when presenting dashboards

Applying the Right Function to Your Calculations

I am often asked if I can give some advice on which functions are best to use when modeling and which ones should be avoided. This then leads to conversations on which functions are best for specific calculations.

You may be surprised by my response to these questions. I believe that there really are no answers because, unfortunately, not every calculation is identical. This is one reason why Excel has so many functions capable of achieving solutions for the equivalent calculation. Numerous functions are needed, because there are subtle differences that can have a significant effect on the result. With so many functions available, hopefully there should always be one that meets the modeler's needs.

Now that I have burst that bubble, let's look at the positive. While I cannot give definitive answers as to which are the right functions to apply to calculations, I can tell why certain functions work better than others for specific calculations.

Functions That Look Up Information

The majority of calculations that are used in models are based on the lookup; that is, by using a key or reference you can unlock further details that can then be substitutes and used through the calculation. There are several lookup functions, and some are more specialized for specific types of calculations. For instance, the function =GETPIVOTDATA is designed purely for getting information from a pivot table and will not work properly unless it's applied to a pivot table.

There following three lookup functions are ones that all modelers should be familiar with:

- =VLOOKUP()
- =MATCH()
- =INDEX()

In addition, the VLOOKUP() is also partnered by the HLOOKUP() function, and the MATCH function is generally combined with INDEX() to for an INDEX() MATCH() formula. In Chapter 3, these functions were covered. If you are unclear on how to use them, turn back to that chapter and refresh your memory. The best way to learn these functions is to actually practice them. Get a worksheet and carefully go through writing the syntax, even with minimal data, just to begin to understand how the functions work and to start becoming comfortable with using them.

I have one final note about these three functions. I always prefer to use the INDEX() MATCH() combination in contrast to VLOOKUPS, although this is a matter of preference. There are a number of potential issues in relation to computer processing capability with VLOOKUPS that steer me away from using it.

Functions That Require a Condition

For calculations where a specific condition must be reached in order to get the correct result, the majority of go-to functions include the following:

- =IF()
- =SUMIF()
- =COUNTIF()
- =SUMIFS()
- =AVERAGEIF()

Do not allow yourself to go through this book without knowing how to use the =IF() and =SUMIF() functions. They are the most important condition-driven functions you will ever get to use. In order to build a serious model, these will be your most useful functions for calculations reliant on the data held in another cell or when you require input from the model user. (Again, these functions were covered in Chapter 3.)

Functions That Are Driven by Dates

Dates and times are always tricky because they just don't work on a typical denary level, and so require some conversions. In other words, if you try to add two dates together, the result will not be as you expect unless they are converted. In almost every model you create, you will need at least one of the following functions when working with dates:

- =DATEVALUE()
- =EOMONTH()
- =WORKDAY()
- =WEEKDAY()
- =TODAY()
- =DAYS360()
- =YEAR()
- =MONTH()

All of these functions are crucial in one way or another. You will seriously limit your ability to creating efficient, fast, and clear calculations if you neglect to use any of these functions.

Functions for Precise Situations

Excel is seen as a financial application in many quarters and is really the most widely used application in finance circles today. One ironic aspect of Excel is that many of the popular financial functions have some odd quirks or just don't feel complete. In other words, you generally need to have strong financial background in order to use them. This brings us to our next point—many of these functions can be created in other ways, which means they have alternatives. There are a clutch of functions that have no alternatives and are used in precise situations that should be understood by modelers. The functions that you should always be able to use:

- =DB()
- =DDB()
- =IRR()
- =XIRR()
- =NPV()
- =XNPV()
- =SLN()
- =SYD()
- =FV()

For instance, the DB(), DDB(), SYD(), and SLN() functions are all about calculating depreciation, while the NPV(), XNPV(), IRR(), and XIRR() are for capital budgeting. However, you should still be familiar with how they work and be capable of applying them to calculations that demand that particular situation.

Mathematical Functions

All calculations are mathematical in one way or another, so why are some calculations described as specifically being mathematical? The reason why some of the functions are called mathematical is that they are designed to simulate a specific mathematical problem or solution. For instance, the SUM() function is mathematical because it is designed to calculate the total of a range of cells.

When discussing mathematical functions in Excel, I am referring to functions that are built around particular math problems and their solutions. These functions are often too limited for general modeling, but there are some that have some major uses in modeling. Yes, you could get by without them, but you will find that having them greatly enhances your ability to create good calculations. Here is a list of the most commonly used mathematical functions in models:

- =MOD()
- =ABS()
- =CEILING()
- =INT()
- =RANDBETWEEN()
- =ROUND()
- =ROUNDUP()
- =ROUNDDOWN()
- =SUM()
- =SUMIF()
- =SUMPRODUCT()
- =SUMIFS()
- =SUBTOTAL()

You will immediately spot that a number of the functions appeared previously in other sections of this chapter, such as the SUMIF function. These functions operate on calculations in several ways, and so there are some that can be considered conditional or mathematical. Aside from the massive importance of SUM(), which cannot be understated; SUMPRODUCT() is another must-know function because it saves an enormous amount of time and effort when used correctly. All of these functions mentioned in this and the previous sections should be part of the modeler's armory, and not one should be neglected.

Functions Dependent on Text

In an ideal world, you wouldn't need text functions in Excel because after all Excel is not a word or text tool. However, the reality is text is part of the data and information that modelers routinely work with. Being able to do even relatively simple calculations like extracting the last name from a lump of text is very important. This list of text functions is critical to know because you will always need them in a model and they will save you time:

- =FIND()
- =LEFT()
- =MID()
- =RIGHT()
- =LEN()
- =REPLACE()
- =TEXT()
- =TRIM()
- =VALUE()

Without exception, all of the listed functions are critical to know because they help you deal with the more common problems that afflict modelers. For example, these functions can correct the data that is inconsistent from row to row, or when you need to extract first names and last names and some of the names have middle names and others do not.

Calculations Involving Logical and Information Functions

Logical functions are about adding functionality rather than making pure calculations, and so they are not always critical. However, being capable of building error checking and being competent to work with unknown issues is what differentiates good modeling from standard modeling. These functions should also be part of the modeler's kit:

- =IF()
- =AND()
- =FALSE()
- =TRUE()
- =NOT()
- =OR()
- =ISERROR()
- =ISBLANK()

- =ISTEXT()
- =ISNUMBER()
- =CELL()

Linking Your Calculations to Inputs and Outputs

We have previously looked at how the calculations link the inputs to the outputs by bringing into the calculation worksheet the input links.[1] Then the calculations were created, which are then picked up by the outputs as links.

All that can be said is that the outputs should not have any calculations. They should be purely linkages to the calculation.

Case Study: Math in Modeling

How much of financial modeling is about math? Or to put it another way, does the modeler need to have an above average grasp of math to succeed? These questions are valid and also have a lot of gravity, mainly since modeling has yet to be defined. Does it fall into the category of science, business, IT, mathematics, engineering, or commerce? Because so many modelers have accounting backgrounds, it does seem as if modeling falls somewhere between business and math, but I am not convinced on that score.

In this case study, I will discuss math—specifically how much math is involved in modeling and what aspects of math should the modeler be ready to apply. In order to investigate this topic, a few examples of calculations and solutions that are commonplace in modeling will be discussed. Before launching into the examples, I want to first explain one aspect about modeling and math: BODMAS.

BODMAS

BODMAS stands for BRACKETS, ORDER (Power), DIVISION, MULTIPLICATION, ADDITION, SUBTRACTION. This is the foundation of how to perform calculation orders in mathematics, and this is how Excel will always interpret calculations. Therefore, it makes sense that modeling would use the same order. So with BODMAS, how would you order a calculation?

---

[1]For more about inputs and outputs, see chapters 7 and 10 in Jack Avon *The Handbook of Financial Modeling* (Apress, 2013).

In the United States, this can also be referred to as PEMDAS: PARENTHESIS, EXPONENTS, MULTIPLICATION and DIVISION, ADDITION, and SUBTRACTION.

$$4 + 8 \times 2 - 10 \times 6/2$$

The simplest way to solve this equation is to look for the order of BODMAS in relation to the calculation.

BRACKETS	None
ORDER	None
DIVISION	6/2 = 3
MULTIPLICATION	8 x 2, 10 x 3
ADDITION	4 + 16
SUBTRACTION	20 – 30

Because this may still feel complicated, let's go a step further. The BRACKETS part is very important because it is the first operation that will be executed. As long as you use brackets, you can force the order to execute how you want. When creating calculations that have a mix of operators, always use the brackets to control the order. From a modeling standpoint, this is good practice because it then becomes clearer exactly which operations are executed first to last. For the previous equation, rewrite it this way:

$$(4 + 8 \times 2) - (10 \times 6/2)$$

This will give us this equation:

$$8 \times 2 = 16 + 4 = 20 - 6/2 = 3 \times 10 = 30$$

$$20 - 30 = -10$$

Understanding BODMAS and correctly applying this order is so critical to modeling calculations. If this subject is difficult for you to understand, purchase a math book and make the effort to gain a solid understanding of it. Excel will always use the BODMAS order to evaluate calculations. If you are unclear on this order, the results from your formula calculations will not match expectations. And because your understanding of the orders is unclear, you will be unaware that the calculation is wrong.

The Math in Modeling

Fortunately, there is not a lot of math that the modeler needs to apply because most of it is already captured in the functions. It may surprise you that I know many modelers who do not have a mathematical background and actually consider themselves weak in math, but nonetheless they are modelers. The main difference is that they are comfortable around numbers and are not overawed by them. The math that comes in modeling is the ability to perform calculations and recognize the functions that are most appropriate, like those in Figures 8-5a and 8-5b.

Cells that sum totals

SUMIF()	Gives the total for a range cell with one condition		
SUMIFS()	Gives the total for a range of cells with more than one condition		
SUMPRODUCT()	Multiplies the elements of one or more arrays		
SUM()	Gives the total for a range of cells an the sums or adds the products together.		
SUBTOTAL()	Gives the sub total of a range of cells using anyone of the eleven pre-set calculations.		
		Function Number	Pre-set calculations
		1	AVERAGE
		2	COUNT
		3	COUNTA
		4	MAX
		5	MIN
		6	PRODUCT
		7	STDEV
		8	STDEVP
		9	SUM
		10	VAR
		11	VARP
AVERAGE()	Gives the arithmetic mean for a set of numbers in a range of cells.		
AVERAGEIF()	Gives the arithmetic mean for a set of numbers in a range of cells that match a given		

Figure 8-5a. There are number of functions that sum cell ranges, and each should be applied against structure of the model calculations

Cells that count ranges

COUNT()	Counts the cells in range that contain numbers only.
COUNTA()	Counts the cells in range that contain data.
COUNTIF()	Counts the cells in range that fulfil given condition

Arithmetic

+
-
/
*

Figure 8-5b. This figure shows the count functions and arithmetic that will be required in the majority of models

Making Checks in Models

The making of checks shows that the numbers in the model add up properly and with integrity. The checks should also be used to alert the model user to issues with the model when numbers are not matching the checksum. Creating the checks is where modelers will need to apply as much of their own math knowledge as possible. This part is about testing that the calculations and formula are working accurately and relies on the modeler interpreting what constitutes an adequate check as can be seen in Figure 8-6.

	C6		fx =SUM(D6:O6)=0												
	B	C	D	E	F	G	H	I	J	K	L	M	N	O
Date from			01-Jan-2014	01-Feb-2014	01-Mar-2014	01-Apr-2014	01-May-2014	01-Jun-2014	01-Jul-2014	01-Aug-2014	01-Sep-2014	01-Oct-2014	01-Nov-2014	01-Dec-2014
Date To			31-Jan-2014	28-Feb-2014	31-Mar-2014	30-Apr-2014	31-May-2014	30-Jun-2014	31-Jul-2014	31-Aug-2014	30-Sep-2014	31-Oct-2014	30-Nov-2014	31-Dec-2014
Cash flow			36,000	36,004	36,001	36,002	36,010	36,003	35,994	35,998	35,991	35,995	35,990	35,991
Working Capital			36,000	36,003	36,001	36,002	36,010	36,003	35,994	35,998	35,991	35,995	35,990	35,991
Check		FALSE			1									

Figure 8-6. Simple financial checks are about math

Adapting Math Functions

There are two math-based functions that I find extremely useful. The first is the ABS() function, which stands for Absolute. This function turns any number to a positive and allows the modeler to continue to use a number irrespective of whether it's a positive or negative. This function becomes useful when creating outputs that have to be in a standard format, although that format may not conform the way the model has been built. For instance, in an income statement, the revenue is credit and so is a negative, and the expenses are debits and are positive. These may be modeled in this way, but the outputs might need to show all the numbers as positive. This is when the ABS() function becomes useful (see Figure 8-7.)

	C6		fx =ABS(C4)+ABS(C5)											
	B	C	D	E	F	G	H	I	J	K	L	M	N
Date from		01-Jan-2014	01-Feb-2014	01-Mar-2014	01-Apr-2014	01-May-2014	01-Jun-2014	01-Jul-2014	01-Aug-2014	01-Sep-2014	01-Oct-2014	01-Nov-2014	01-Dec-2014
Date To		31-Jan-2014	28-Feb-2014	31-Mar-2014	30-Apr-2014	31-May-2014	30-Jun-2014	31-Jul-2014	31-Aug-2014	30-Sep-2014	31-Oct-2014	30-Nov-2014	31-Dec-2014
Positive responses		12	16	13	14	22	15	6	10	3	5	2	3
Negative responses		(12)	(22)	(23)	(19)	(16)	(18)	(24)	(23)	(30)	(28)	(43)	(41)
Total responses		24	38	36	33	38	33	30	33	35	33	45	44

Figure 8-7. The ABS() function is used to provide a total response

The other math function is MOD(); this function gives the result of the remainder when a number is divided by a divisor. For instance, if you have a number five and the divisor is two, you divide the five by the two.

$$5/2 = 2 \text{ remainders } 1$$

The MOD() function in this case will return a one. This innocuous function may seem of little use, but it has real value when you need a mechanism that can activate and deactivate a calculation based on a result. I use MOD() mainly for creating timelines and time period—which are activated by a specific user input. In Figure 8-8, the formula is looking for the remainder after dividing the period with the number 12.

	C5			f_x	=IF(MOD(C4,12)=0,12,MOD(C4,12))									
	A	B	C	D	E	F	G	H	I	J	K	L	M	N
1														
2	Date from		01-Jan-2014	01-Feb-2014	01-Mar-2014	01-Apr-2014	01-May-2014	01-Jun-2014	01-Jul-2014	01-Aug-2014	01-Sep-2014	01-Oct-2014	01-Nov-2014	01-Dec-2014
3	Date To		31-Jan-2014	28-Feb-2014	31-Mar-2014	30-Apr-2014	31-May-2014	30-Jun-2014	31-Jul-2014	31-Aug-2014	30-Sep-2014	31-Oct-2014	30-Nov-2014	31-Dec-2014
4	Period		1	2	3	4	5	6	7	8	9	10	11	12
5	Month In Year		1	2	3	4	5	6	7	8	9	10	11	12
6														

Figure 8-8. This model uses the MOD() function to calculate the month in the year

While financial modeling requires an understanding and healthy respect for math, there is no reason why a modeler who does not have a math background should not prevail. The math that is used in modeling is applicable to the models that are being built and so can be learned. However, having said that, there is no reason for not having a sound grasp of basic arithmetic and understanding arithmetic ordering. There are definite advantages to having a more mathematical grasp when building quantitative models such as Monte Carlo or Black-Scholes, but even with those models most of the math can be learned while modeling.

Keyboard Shortcuts

Provided is a table of Excel keyboard shortcuts. This is not a full list of short-cuts but is a selection based on their relevancy for modeling. The best method of learning these shortcuts is to refer to this appendix as you use Excel to tackle a situation.

Alt + =	Insert the SUM formula
Alt + FI	Insert a Chart Sheet
Alt + FII	Display the VB Editor
Alt + F8	Display the Macro dialog box
Alt + Shift + FI	Insert worksheet
FI	Open online Help or the Office Assistant
F2	Edit active cell
F5	Go to
F7	Check spelling
F9	Calculate all sheets
FII	Create chart
Shift + F2	Edit cell comment
Shift + F3	Insert a function into a formula
Shift + F5	Search

(continued)

Shift + F9	Calculate active worksheet
Shift + F10	Display shortcut menu
Shift + Space	Select entire row
Shift + arrow key	Extend selection by one cell
Ctrl + ; (semicolon)	Insert current date.
Ctrl + 9	Hide row
Ctrl + C	Copy selected area
CTRL + END	Move to the end of the spreadsheet
Ctrl + F1	Search
Ctrl + F12	Open
Ctrl + K	Insert hyperlink
Ctrl + N	New workbook
Ctrl + O	Open
Ctrl + P	Print
Ctrl + Arrow key	Move to the edge of the current data region
Ctrl+ R	Cells to copy cell contents from left
Ctrl + Shift + Enter	Enter a formula as an array formula
Ctrl + Shift + Space	Select all cells
Ctrl + Shift + O	Select all cells with comments
Ctrl + Shift + arrow key	Extend the selection to the last nonblank cell
Ctrl +V	Paste from Clipboard
Ctrl +Y	Repeat the last action
Ctrl + Z	Undo the last action

I

Index

Get the eBook for only $10!

Now you can take the weightless companion with you anywhere, anytime. Your purchase of this book entitles you to 3 electronic versions for only $10.

This Apress title will prove so indispensible that you'll want to carry it with you everywhere, which is why we are offering the eBook in 3 formats for only $10 if you have already purchased the print book.

Convenient and fully searchable, the PDF version enables you to easily find and copy code—or perform examples by quickly toggling between instructions and   applications. The MOBI format is ideal for your Kindle, while the ePUB can be utilized on a variety of mobile devices.

Go to www.apress.com/promo/tendollars to purchase your companion eBook.

Other Apress Business Titles You Will Find Useful

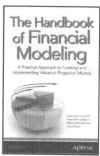
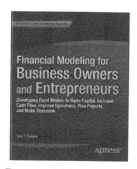

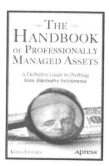

46354673R00140

Made in the USA
San Bernardino, CA
04 March 2017